James Wallace Darrow

Five Hundred Questions and Answers!

on poultry raising - A book of practical and authenic information in the

form of questions and answers on various subjects, as feed and care,

diseases, eggs, incubators, buildings, etc. - Vol. 1

James Wallace Darrow

Five Hundred Questions and Answers!
on poultry raising - A book of practical and authenic information in the form of questions and answers on various subjects, as feed and care, diseases, eggs, incubators, buildings, etc. - Vol. 1

ISBN/EAN: 9783337291747

Printed in Europe, USA, Canada, Australia, Japan

Cover: Foto ©Andreas Hilbeck / pixelio.de

More available books at **www.hansebooks.com**

FIVE HUNDRED
QUESTIONS...
and ANSWERS

—— ON ——

POULTRY RAISING.

——— •◆• ———

A Book of Practical Authentic Information In the Form of
Questions and Answers on Various Subjects, as
Feed and Care, Diseases, Eggs, Incubators
Buildings, Etc., with a Chapter on
Turkeys, Geese and Ducks.

——— •◆• ———

BY J. W. DARROW.

——— •◆• ———

CHATHAM, N. Y.
J. WALLACE DARROW.
1899.

TABLE OF CONTENTS.

CHAPTER 1.

Feeding and Care.

Flaxseed, Sorghum, Etc.—Are the seeds here named good for fowls?

Flaxseed meal may be fed in small quantity, but it should be used with discretion. A gill to 10 hens in soft food, twice or three times a week is sufficient, as it is somewhat laxative. Sorghum seed is a good feed and may be fed almost as freely as corn. Broom corn seed is excellent and may be fed every other day in winter.

Vegetables for Winter.—I wish to devote a portion of my garden to raising some vegetables to feed my poultry next winter. What would you advise?

Cabbage and turnips; getting a good winter variety of the former,—Drumheads or Sureheads;—and the purple top strap leaf turnips. These can be sown as late as July, where early peas and early potatoes have come out. Clover hay cut fine and steamed, is far superior to cabbage, turnips, etc. It seems to be exactly the thing wanted, the cabbage, etc,, being a makeshift.

Onions and Eggs.—My fowls love onions, but it is said that onions give the eggs an onion flavor. Do they?

No; onions do not affect the flavor of the eggs. Onions have been fed for weeks at a time along with other food, with no taint perceptible in the eggs. It would be just as reasonable to say that chicks hatched from eggs laid by onion eating hens would smell and taste of the onion! A difference in food no doubt affects the color of the yolk; the eggs from hens fed on corn have a deeper and richer colored yolk than the eggs of hens fed strictly on nitrogenous foods. Fowls that have free range eat everything that a crow will eat, and yet their eggs do not taste of garbage or carrion. Onions are a healthful food for fowls, often better than medicine.

Feeding Oats.—Are oats a good grain for fowls?

Oats may be used as a portion of the ration for poultry the year round, and especially for the large Asiatic varieties that are predisposed to put on an excess of fat when fed in the ordinary way. But we would recommend that the oats be good and sound, and first-class in quality, otherwise they will not do as a constant feed.

Carbonaceous Foods.—Please give a list of the foods which are carbonaceous and of those which are nitrogenous. Which of the above are for bone and feathers and which are for fat and muscle?

Carbonaceous foods are the grains, with fat of any kind, as well as potatoes and other starchy foods. Nitrogeneous foods are milk, meat, beans, clover and the grasses. The nitrogenous form bone, feathers, and muscle. The carbonaceous form fat. All foods, however, are to a certain extent both carbonaceous and nitrogenous, hence a list could not be well arranged.

How Often to Feed.—Would you advise the feeding of fowls three times a day, when they are enclosed in yards, during the winter months, when the days are so short?

When fowls are inclosed, with no exercise, they are liable to become over fat. The proper method is to feed only twice a day. In the morning give about a quart of grain to 15 hens, scattered in litter, and compel them to scratch and work for it. At night give the same quantity. If fed too frequently they will expect to receive food, and will not work, following the attendant constantly. Of course when we mention grain, we refer not to grain only, but a variety of feed.

Sun Flower Seeds.—Are sun flower seeds good for poultry?

Yes. Feed a pint, three times a week, to 12 hens, and they will be found excellent. They are very nitrogenous and also rich in fats.

Sugar-Cane Seed, Etc.—What properties are claimed in the sugar-cane seed, and with what grain does it compare best—wheat or corn? Will sweet skimmed milk answer the place of fresh meat for young chicks?

It approaches more to wheat than to corn, but is more nitrogenous than corn. The skimmed milk will not take the place of meat, but is excellent. Give any amount they will drink of the milk.

Beef Blood.—Is beef blood good for chickens, and how is it best prepared?

Beef blood is excellent, being rich in nitrogen, and nearly approaches the white of the egg in composition. It may be thickened with a mixture of meal and bran, put in a bag and boiled, or it may be mixed, if fresh, with the regular soft food. Feed it only twice or three times a week.

Curing and Feeding Clover.—When should clover be cut, and do you make it in hay or pack it away in boxes while green? Do you steam it before feeding?

Clover should be cut when the blossoms begin to turn brown. It is then at its best with the seed-making material stored up in the stalk. It can be siloed in boxes or barrels, but probably the most convenient way of keeping it is to make it into hay, and when wanted to feed, run it through a hay-cutter or clover-cutter, cutting it into about half-inch lengths, and steam in a closed vessel. Siloed clover is no doubt better if it is perfectly siloed, but we would advise anyone inexperienced in siloing to experiment with a small quantity first, making hay his chief reliance. Some poultrymen fill a huge kettle with clover, pour on a couple of buckets of hot water, and put a slow fire under it to keep up the steaming and bring to a boil, then stirring in meal and sorts to make a mash. Excellent results are also obtained by simply cutting up the clover into a firkin or tub, pouring boiling hot water onto it, letting it steam (covered closely) all night. This, fed clear, is very like the grass that biddy gets when running at large, and is an excellent green feed.

Beans for Fowls—Are Red Kidney beans cooked and mixed with ground feed good for hens that lay?

They are excellent, being highly nitrogenous, but too expensive for the purpose as compared with grain.

Coal Ashes—Is it a good plan to keep a supply of coal ashes before hens so they can pick them, eat all they desire, and wallow in them?

Use coal ashes, but first sift them. The fowls will eat a great deal of the course stuff in the dust and ashes.

Meat Scraps.—Are the meat scraps where tallow is pressed out good for chickens? Or is that good where lard is pressed out by the butchers?

As the grease is usually very thoroughly extracted by pressure and heat, the scraps may not contain much fat. They may be used if not fed in excess.

Feeding Ten Hens.—I have ten hens, and can feed them three times a day,—morning, noon and night. What in your judgment should I feed them?

You will probably find the plan of using cut clover, (scalded) sprinkled with meal, excellent in the morning, with wheat at night. A mash of cooked vegetables, corn meal, fine feed and shorts, with a handful of ground beef scrap for animal food, also gives a very perfect ration and a variety. We advise feeding this only once a day, grain at other times.

Green Oats and Rye.—Are green oats as good as clover hay for hens, and, what time ought they to be cut? Is rye good also?

When young grass, rye or oats are cut before making much growth they are watery and contain little nutrition; too much of such feed causes the hens to have scours. Many persons have been disappointed in confining their fowls on young rye or an exclusive feed. It is excellent as a dietary food, but all very young grass is mostly water. We do not advise cutting such for winter use, but if oats are grown and the crop cut when the grain is in the milky stage, near the stage of maturity, the nutritive matter, on its way to fill the grain, will be arrested in the stalk, so that, when cured, the whole stalk (with the grain) if cured, stored in the barn, and cut with a fine cutter. will make excellent feed for the hens. The oats should be cut green, just as the seed heads begin to form. No green feed equals clover, however.

Young Calves Meat.—Will it pay to use the meat of young calves for poultry? If so, how should it be prepared?

Prepare it by cooking to a broth and thicken with meal and ground oats It is always a good ration for fowls, but ground bone and meat is superior.

Buttermilk.—Is the buttermilk beneficial or injurious to poultry? If not injurious will all they want hurt them?

It is excellent. Give them all they wish of fresh milk, sour milk, buttermilk or milk in any form. For chicks use only the fresh milk.

Carrots as Feed.—Are carrots as good as hay feed for hens, either boiled, mashed and mixed with wheat middlings, or should they be chopped fine and fed raw?

Carrots are a good vegetable feed either cooked or raw. There is no need to chop them fine to feed raw. Split them in halves and the fowls will eat the meat all out of them.

Gravel.—Why is gravel recommended for fowls?

The gravel serves as teeth in the gizzard and assists in grinding and pulverizing the food. The lack of a proper ground diet often causes bowel troubles in fowls, hence gravel, hard bone, or some sharp substances, should always be within reach of the fowls.

General Feeding.——Tell use in a general way how to feed laying hens !

Keep in view the fact that when a hen is laying she is a *producer*, hence when a number of hens are together, and some are not laying, the non laying hens may become too fat, not being required to utilize materials in producing eggs, it is best, therefore, to separate the layers from the others. In the morning give all the cut clover hay (scalded) they will eat. At night give a pound of cut fresh meat and bone to 16 hens, with all the oats, wheat or corn that they will eat.

Feeding Timothy, Rye, Etc.—How about the use of Timothy (or Herdsgrass) as a green food for poultry in winter? It seems to be tender and nice, and not affected by frosts. Would it be better than the steamed clover hay? Are turnip top leaves good to feed hens?

Yes, it would be one of the best of green feeds, and nearly equal to steamed clover hay. Turnip tops are also good, but not equal to fresh grass.

Feed for Chicks.—What kind of feed is best for young chicks when their feathers begin to grow rapidly?

Give a little chopped lean meat, cooked, three times a week; keep pin-head oatmeal before them all the time, also cooked potatoes, turnips or anything that they will eat. A small box of ground bone should be within access.

Bone Meal—Please tell me how to feed bone meal to the chickens; what proportion to feed to pullets and old hens?

It is usual to allow one pound of bone meal or ground meat to 16 fowls, and it may be mixed with other food. A little box of bone-meal may be kept before them all the time, if preferred, as they will not consume more than they desire.

Green Feeds.—We often speak of green feeds. What would you class under this head?

The list comprises grass and grass seed, green corn, ensilage, cabbage, clover, purslane, young beets, garlic, onions, leeks, lettuce, turnips, pumpkins, apples, kohl rabi and carrots.

Hash for Poultry.—What ingredients are best to use in a poultry hash?

It may be made out of meat boiled and minced, mashed potatoes, wheat bran, corn meal and oat meal, with a slight sprinkling of bone dust, the whole mixed with the liquor the meat was boiled in. Chandlers' scraps soaked over night in cold water and afterward minced, may serve in the place of meat.

Feeding Mixed Grain.—Would you advise feeding grains mixed or separately?

All grains should be scattered in litter, such as leaves or cut straw, so as to compel the birds to scratch for them, and also to prevent the greedy hens from robbing those that are timid. It is advisable to change the feed by giving wheat one day, corn the next, and oats the next. Sorghum seed, sunflower seed, buckwheat, or barley may also have places in the rotation.

Length of Cut Clover.—Would you please tell me what is the proper length to cut clover?

For fowls do not cut in lengths longer than half an inch—the shorter the better. It is an excellent ration and fowls love it greatly.

Raw Meat.—Having had poor luck with my hens in hatching this spring, I thought I would ask you if it is injurious to feed raw meat to hens whose eggs are to be used for hatching?

The raw meat, if lean, should be given three times a week. It will not affect the hatching of the eggs. Half an ounce for each hen is enough.

Feed for Light Brahmas.—I have thirteen Light Brahma Hens. They are all well, but do not lay. Can you tell me what is the best feed for them, and what proportion to feed?

The Brahma is somewhat indolent in disposition, and becomes fat very readily. When they appear in perfect health, and do not lay, feed oats, wheat, and meat occasionally.

Charcoal.—What are the benefits to be derived from feeding charcoal?

Charcoal serves more as a corrective than any other purpose, as it is not digestible, being one of the most insoluble substances known. It should always be freshly burned before using it. It corrects acidity and also partially serves as grit.

Clover Ensilage, Etc.—Is clover ensilage good for laying hens in the winter? Is it better than clover hay cut fine and fed? Can it be fed to young chicks without injury, provided it is sweet? Are sugar beets a good winter feed for fowls in confinement?

Clover ensilage is excellent for fowls in winter; it being more succulent than cured hay, it makes a better feed. Young chicks will receive no injury from it if fed intelligently. The beets make a very good winter relish.

To Make Grit.—Will ground bone answer for grit? Will granulated charcoal act in any measure as grit? Would our common granite, pounded or ground, be as good, or better, than gravel or sand?

Ground bone makes excellent grit, as it is hard and sharp, but flint, or some very hard substance is better. Pounded glass, broken china, or any sharp substance, may also be used. Charcoal is rather too soft and is used more as a corrective of bowel disorder.

Wet Feeds.—Is it well to feed wet foods? how do they effect fowls?

Too wet feed causes diarrhœa, dilutes the intestinal juices too much and soon knocks the chickens off their legs. A good dough may be made of corn meal, oat meal, wheat bran and boiled vegetables mashed in the proportion of one third of each, and wet with milk or water, the former preferred. Wet feed may be occasionally allowed as a variety, but *dry feed* is always better.

The Grain Ration.—How much grain should be given 18 hens for dinner and supper?

We would not advise a noon meal. The regular allowance, (or estimate) of grain is one quart per day for 12 hens, with other food as a variety, but no estimate can really be made, as no two hens are alike. Some will consume twice as much as others, and a laying hen requires more meat than the non-layer. If too much grain is eaten the hen may become too fat to lay. An excellent way to estimate is to allow four ounces of *mixed* food (grain, clover, cabbage, etc.) for each fowl.

Feeding for Fattening.—When is the proper time to begin to feed fowls for fattening?

Fattening must not be begun until the fowl has attained its full growth, as growing animals or birds do not fatten as readily as adults, although of course all extra food that will be digested is never lost. The pullets are best taken before they have begun to lay; the male birds when their tails begin to turn, that is when the two sickle feathers begin to top the straight feathers of the tail. The average age will be four months in summer and five to six in winter, but will be early according as the previous feeding has or has not been judiciously generous.

Feeding Chicks.—What is the best feed to give young chicks, say until they are four or six weeks old? Is there any danger of over-feeding chicks of that age, or is it proper to keep a dish of cracked wheat or corn before them all the time? Is sweet milk, butter-milk or curds good for chicks? In fattening chickens for market, what kind of feeding gives the best results?

The first feed should be pin head oat meal, varied with cooked ground grain (or bread), and then mixed grain, such as wheat and cracked corn, (as soon as they can eat it) with mashed potatoes fed every two hours the first week, then four times a day. Also give a little meat three times a week. We do not think you can feed growing chicks too much. The sweet milk etc., is good if fresh. Plenty of cracked corn and mashed potatoes are good for fattening chicks. Young chicks require neither feed nor drink on the day on which they are hatched; in fact, both are injurious, as they interfere with the natural digestion of the yolk, which is absorbed into the bowels at the period of hatching and consti-tutes the first feed.

Bones as a Poultry Feed.—With corn at $1.50 per bushel, what do you consider the value of green bone as poultry feed after it has passed through a bone cutter?

When corn reaches $1.50 per bushel feed may be considered high. The usual estimated allowance of corn, or its equivalent, for a hen, for one year. is five pecks, valued where corn is worth $1.50 per bushel, at $1.87½. At about 20 cents per dozen for eggs (as an average price) a hen must lay 10 dozen eggs a year, to give a profit on the feed, and when the estimate is made for a whole flock the probability is that nine dozen eggs per year will be nearer the number. Green bones, cut (they cannot be ground,) contain meat, oil and phosphate of lime. The bones also contain a considerable propor-tion of nitrogen independent of the adhering meat, cartilage and mar-row. As they differ in composition from grain, a proper comparison is not easily made between the two, especially as much depends on the kind of bones, and the amount of meat adhering to them, and whether it is fat or lean. Bones are more concentrated food than grain, about one ounce of cut bone being con-sidered a fair allowance for each hen per day, or about 23 pounds per year.

The bones alone are not sufficient, as the fowls will need also grain and green feed, but bones may assist in reducing the quantity of grain re-quired. Grain is not a complete feed either, and in feeding bones or other feed, the allowance of five pecks of corn is reduced in propor-tion to the amount of other feed given as a substitute The value of 23 pounds of green bones depends upon the locality. We buy them from the butcher at two cents per pound, but probably could not get them at all if there were a strong competition to secure them. The labor of grinding the bones is also an item, but cut bones just as they come from the mill, and as fine as sausage meat, are now on the mar-ket, in small boxes, at five cents per pound. At this price the 23 pounds would be valued at $1.15, which would be cheaper than corn at $1.87½ for five pecks. The bone being more concentrated (containing less water than corn) is really more val-uable, bulk for bulk, than corn. Leaving out the labor of grinding, the bones are valued at 46 cents. This estimate is made for a year's supply of corn and of bones. It must not be overlooked that bones alone will not answer. Five pecks of corn a year is an allowance of about three ounces per day to each hen. By reducing the amount of grain to 1½ ounces, and the amount of bone to half an ounce, the pro-portions will be fair, but of course, in feeding, it is to be considered that the hen requires less help in the shape of food in summer; green food is also a factor, and the condition and breed of the hens are very important considerations to say nothing of the fact that appe-tites differ, and that individual characteristics must be observed.

Miscellaneous Inquiries.

What shall I feed molting hens? (Give a variety of food. Meat and bone twice a week. A teaspoonful of linseed meal in the grain daily.) Is buckwheat bran good for chicks when wet up? (Yes.) Are refuse crackers good for fowls? (Excellent.) How will it do to feed fowls with bran, mixed with potatoes? (It is excellent.) Is bran, cornmeal and ground feed, mixed with water, good for a morning feed? (Yes.) Is popcorn equal to corn as food for fowls and chicks? (Yes, better, as it contains more nitrogen and phosphates.) Is stove coal and cinders from the stove good for laying hens? (Of no value except for the hens to pick over for grit.) Would crushed cuttle bone (same as used for canary birds) be of any benefit to chickens? Would it be a substitute for ordinary bone? (It is of no value.) Is the small white clover as good as the red for use in feeding poultry? (Yes; it is fully equal to the red.) Is the refuse from a distillery good for chickens? Rye is what they use. (If fed moderately it is excellent.) Should buckwheat be fed whole or ground? (Either mode will answer, but it is usually fed whole.) How could a person keep green clover enough to feed 400 chickens all winter? (You cannot well keep it green without the use of the silo.) Is brewery grain injurious for hens to eat? Also cracked acorns, which they like so much. (Not injurious if fed moderately.) Is lettuce good for young chickens or will it make them sleepy and dumpish? (Excellent) Will cotton-seed meal, if fed to fowls too much, cause the eggs to fail to hatch? (It is fattening, but being of a constipating tendency is seldom used.) Is water-cress good for fowls? (Yes: Excellent.)

Feeding Condensed in a Nutshell.

Avoid tonics, condition powders, etc., in the poultry yard.

Always keep your hens at work. An ideal hen is never a good layer.

Good warm shelter saves feed, and the better is the cheaper and the lower its cost.

Fresh meat and bone, cut with a bone cutter, will make hens lay when all other feeds fail. Give warm water, three times a day, in winter. It is invigorating, and is superior to tonics.

Grain is deficient in lime and mineral matter, but bran is rich in nitrogen, carbon and mineral matter.

Linseed and cotton seed (cake or meal) is excellent given occasionally.

More damage is done by overfeeding than from roosting in the trees and allowing no food. Both are extremes.

Beans and peas, cooked and thickened with bran, and fed twice a week, make an excellent feed for laying hens.

The cardinal foods—cut clover hay, meat and bone, and mixed grain, the clover in the morning and the latter at night.

Breed is everything. The machine for converting feed into eggs must be of the best to be had. Anything and everything will not do.

If the hens have a range in the summer they will need no feed at all. It should cost nothing to produce eggs in summer.

When your birds have bowel disease change the feed for a day or two, and change the *grit*. One-half the troubles are from the lack of *sharp*, hard grit.

Cooked turnips or potatoes, with chopped clover, and thickened with ground corn and oats, makes the feed for ducks and geese, and is excellent for hens also.

One quart of grain feed per day, for ten hens, is considered liberal feeding. This is equivalent to five pecks a year to each hen. If grass and meat are fed give only half the grain.

The hen, like the cow, must be given bulky feed. Give her all the chopped clover, scalded, that she can eat. The clover, with one ounce of lean meat per day, will soon *compel* her to lay.

Common fowls are nondescripts, no two being alike. One flock of common fowls may be something different from another. Economize in feed by using the breeds, so as to understand their characteristics.

The ordinary ground meat will keep any length of time. It is the residuum of soap factories after the fat has been extracted under hydraulic pressure, and with the aid of superheated steam.

Separate the layers from the others. You cannot keep old hens, pullets, fat hens, and lean hens together any more than you can keep dry cows, heifers not yet in milk, and fresh cows together, for they do not require the same feed.

Leghorns and Brahmas cannot thrive together. Have your flocks uniform. When you send to a breeder for eggs of pure breeds remember that in that case "eggs are not eggs." It is the *stock* you seek, not eggs particularly. You can get eggs at home, but not stock of the kind you wish.

CHAPTER II.

Diseases of Poultry.

Roup, Its Causes, Symptoms and Treatment.

CAUSES OF ROUP.—Roup has its chief cause in a cold and a cold may be taken in numerous ways, chief of which are draughts of winds blowing *over and upon* the fowls while at roost. Whatever may cause colds, this is true that if neglected they are liable to terminate in roup and when a fowl has roup in earnest, the chanaces are against the fowl's recovery. The proper time to treat a bird for roup is *just before she has it* or in other words treat her on the first appearance of a cold. With proper care, roup need never enter a flock. Prevention is always better than cure.

SYMPTOMS OF ROUP-COLD —These are sneezing, hoarseness, wheezy-breathing, eyes watery with a whitish foamy matter, and a discharge of a watery nature from the nostrils which sometimes hangs in little bubbles on the beak. This is the time to begin the treatment, for the next stage is more serious and may be known by an increased rattling in the throat, yellowish discharge from nostrils which has an offensive odor, swelling of head, eyes closed, ulcerated throat, fever, discoloration of comb, when death is pretty sure to follow.

TREATMENT OF ROUP.—Remedies are numerous though what proves effective in one case may not in another. We have invited some of the most experienced fanciers in the United States to contribute their practical remedies for this disease, for this edition of "Five Hundred Questions and Answers" and we present them in the hope that some one or all may prove helpful to the poultrymen who may have occasion to try them.

Roup, says Stoddard's "Poultry Diseases," is a disease of the lining membrance of the beak, extending, however, to the whole head and throat, through the tear duct to the eye, and finally affecting the whole constitution. In fatal cases death ensues on three to eight days after the specific roup symptoms show themselves, and cases not treated are generally fatal whenever the malady appears as an epidemic in its severe form. After death the gall, bladder and liver are found full of pus; the flesh has a bad odor and is soft, slimy and spongy, especially about the lungs. There are many other names under which this malady is often described; swelled eyes, diphtheria, sore head, hoarseness, bronchitis, asthma, snuffles, canker, blindness, influenza, sore throat, quinsy, etc., but some of these conditions may exist even when roup is not present. The causes of roup, like the causes of cholera, do not all need special enumeration here. Anything that lowers the tone of the fowl, bad food, bad housing, lice, bad ventilation, filthy houses, etc. A very prominent cause, however, is exposure to cold and wet. So prominent is this, and so marked is the commencement of the disease at the beak, that it might almost be called malignant catarrh, and it is possibly nothing more. Influenza in the human being sometimes assumes a distinctive form, and fowls are sometimes destroyed by colds alone. Roup, therefore, is most common in autumn and winter and where fowls are exposed to wet, cold draughts and damp sunless quarters. The disease is contagious, from contact with the discharge, either when a diseased fowl touches another or when a well fowl gets the discharge through the drinking fountain or otherwise. It can also, if brought into contact with the human eye, or with a wound or an abraded surface on the hand, cause serious inflammation, so that caution is needful in handling the fowl.

Symptoms:—It may come on suddenly, or slowly, with previous signs of general debility, moping, etc. The first signs are those of catarrh or cold in the head, dry cough and dull wheezing. Much fever; The fowls drink eagerly. The combs and wattles may be pale or dark colored. The cold grows worse. There is a yellowish discharge, thin and watery at first, which grows thicker and thicker, and fills—in severe cases—throat, nostrels and eyes, the latter being closed and swollen even to the size of a walnut and the sides of the face may swell up. Pustules form all about the head and in the gullet, and discharge a frothy pus. The crop is generally swollen, though not always. The blinded fowls cannot see to eat or drink, and this hastens the fatal end. The discharge has a bad odor, and this is *the one most distinctive symptom* of the roup. The clogging of the nostrils also seriously impedes the breathing. In all this, there does not seem to be any trace of special poison; it is like typhoid influenza. One of the best means of detecting the approach of roup is to lift the wing of the suspected bird and see if there is not a spot there where the feathers are smeared with a discharge from the beak, which has rubbed off when the bird has put its head under its wing at night. Also invariably look at the nostrils and see if they are clean and free from the slightest clogging. Go the rounds at night with a lantern and inspect your birds. Listen then for rattling or sneezing.

Treatment:—First and foremost, put the diseased fowls by themselves, if possible, each one separately. and as to cleaning, etc., proceed exactly as recommended in the treatment of cholera. Take all possible means to prevent any of the discharge coming in contact with any other fowl, which renders thorough purification of the drinking vessels, etc , necessary. Some preparation of carbolic acid is good for this purpose. Give warm, stimulating food, house in a warm, dry place, with a sandy bottom. Various plans are followed for the internal treatment of the sick fowl, most of which are often successful. A mild purge at the beginning, as for instance a spoonful of castor oil is advisable. German Roup Pills are highly recommended. In addition to the above, some stimulants, such as mustard or pulverized ginger in pills as large as a pea, given thrice daily, with cayenne

pepper in the food and water.¶ The rule for pepper in the soft food is to season as strongly as if for human food; in the drink, make it as strong as your own "pepper tea." Dr. Bennett recommends, thrice a day, a pill of the size of a hazelnut made of equal parts of pulverized sulphur, powdered charcoal and new yeast. To this must be added the mustard, etc., stimulants. Powdered charcoal should be added freely to the soft food always in this disease. It purifies the digestive organs against the foul matter in the throat which the patient is obliged to swallow. In any plan of treatment, if the disease runs several days the purge should be repeated. Besides the dosing, the eyes, throat and face must be carefully attended to. Wash the head thoroughly with castile soapsuds, or better, with Labarraque's Solution of Chlorinated Soda, mixed with two parts of water, several times a day if there be much discharge. If the throat be clogged *with the secretion,* clear out and use the *chl. sod.* here also, applying it with a camel's-hair brush. The swelling of the eyes may generally be reduced by a patient bathing, but sometimes an operation is necessary to remove the deposit. Nitric acid, applied with a feather into the nostrils twice or thrice, is sometimes used, taking off the old scab at each application. Do not be in a hurry to return the fowl, after recovery, to the flock.

TREATMENT FOR ROUP, ETC., BY PRACTICAL POULTRYMEN.

The following treatments for the diseases named are recommended by leading fanciers and will be found invaluable. They are written especially for this book. The authors' names are prefixed.

PHILANDER WILLIAMS:—I use camphorated oil for roup and it will cure any case if taken in time. I keep it in a small can with spring bottom and inject the oil in the fowl's nostrils. It is also good for canker. It is well to add 5 drops of carbolic acid to each ounce of camphorated oil.

F. B. ZIMMER:—As soon as I notice the first signs of a "cold" I give one or two doses of cod liver oil and camphor and they "knock it crazy." But if it is neglected for a day or two, *gilithera* and good care saves them.

Good quarters and good care amount to more than a whole drug store of remedies. Cholera and indigestion I prevent by proper care and food.

H. S. BABCOCK:—Under the term "roup" is embraced a variety of diseases ranging from a common cold to a distemper resulting in, to all appearances, blood poisoning. For a cold nothing is better than warm quarters, with a few drops of aconite in the drinking water, the supply being limited in quantity to insure the taking of medicine. For the more violent form of roup I have found nothing better than the external use of bromo-chloralum, diluted one-half in water, bathing the affected parts and also injecting the same up the nostrils. To this treatment I add a liberal use of sulphur in the food, making the food at the same time stimulating in character. Give fullest ventilation and keep quarters clean, dry and warm as possible without fire.

Canker.—Remove the deposits, causing as little bleeding as possible. Touch the affected parts with tincture of iodine. Sulphur is often efficacious in such cases, as also is borax.

E. E. EDWARDS:—For roup take three parts of glycerine, one part of turpentine, mix the two well together, having half-teaspoonful of both. Give part down throat of fowl and rub rest on nostrils. I have treated several fowls this way, it effecting a cure. I treat the fowl when first symptoms appear.

JONES WILCOX:—A valuable remedy for all throat and head troubles (roup in all its forms) is to confine the fowls in hen house and fumigate with pine tar and spirits turpentine in equal parts. Put these in an iron vessel and ignite with a coal of fire or match.

Among other remedies given by writers on the subject in various books and periodicals are the following:

Anoint the fowl's head and neck twice a day for two or three days with strong vinegar. Put logwood in drinking vessels on which pour lukewarm water. Give no other drink. Do not confine too closely.

Stephen Beal in his "Profitable Poultry Keeping" remarks that a cold never becomes roup unless the blood is in a scrofulous condition. Sulphur or charcoal are best to correct the scrofula and copaiba capsules should be used for the cold. Wash head with chlorinated soda. Purify all drinking vessels, etc., with a wash of dilute carbolic acid.

A writer in the "Southern Fancier" says: "If roup is let run until the case is well developed, take alum water as strong as it can well be made, and mix with one third its quantity strong vinegar and wash the head well and see that the nostrils are clear, so the solution can be forced through. This remedy applied once or twice a day will cure ninety-nine out of a hundred cases. Separate all diseased fowls and keep them in a warm place. Burnt alum applied to the sores after scabs are removed will cure canker every time, but must be frequently repeated and well dusted in."

London "Poultry" gives this: Three drops of spirits of camphor put on a piece of bread and fed to roupy fowls produced a cure. Another recipe is a teaspoonful of crude carbolic acid in a pint of water, as a wash. Rub glycerine around eyes. Inject carbolic acid and water with a small syringe.

Mr. C. E. Watson in "New England Fancier" says: A quick and sure cure for roup is as follows: Take a small glass syringe, fill once with clear whiskey and inject in passage from roof of mouth outward through the nostrils. This remedy applied two nights in succession has never failed with me. I used it twice on my best Langshan pullet when she was so far gone she could breathe merely by gasping, and was too weak to stand. I was advised to wring her neck, but in 48 hours she was back in the coop as bright and chipper as ever.

Mr. W. McNeil in "Canadian Poultry Review," says: The best cure I ever found for roup is to take two ounces of the best vinegar, one tablespoonful of pulverized alum, one tablespoonful of sugar of lead; put all into one bottle. Bathe birds' head and nostrils well, night and morning. This will cure the worst case of roup.

The "Poultry Keeper" is a strong advocate of spongia. This is a homeopathic remedy, and comes either as pellets or as the mother tincture. To prevent roup, put five drops of tincture, or fifteen pellets, in a quart of the drinking water and give no other water to drink. For sick birds double the quantity of spongia to the water. There is no handling of the birds. The drinking vessels should be clean.

Another good roup cure is bromochloralum, mixed with equal quantity of water. Ten cents worth is enough to get at one time. With a sewing machine oil can inject two or three drops in each nostril, twice a day, and two or three drops down the throat. Every night give the bird a pill of assafœtida, the size of a grain of corn, and sift a little red pepper on their soft food till birds get better. A similar treatment is to inject into the nostrils five drops of a mixture of bromo-chloralum and water, equal parts, and then pour down the throat a mixture of a teaspoonful of warm lard and two drops carbolic acid.

Roup and cholera are often confounded by the inexperienced. Roup may linger for months, cholera "kills or cures" inside of 36 hours. The difficulty in treating roup is the handling of the birds. The bromochloralum remedy is among the best. Add, also, 40 grains of permangenate of potash to each gallon of the drinking water.

CANKER.

Canker shows itself upon the corners of the mouth usually, at first, and is really one form of roup. Then the yellowish white spots appear upon the face and wattles. It spreads rapidly, however, and we know cases where in thirty-six hours from its first showing the roof of the upper mandible, the tongue and the nostrils were completely covered with this offensive and troublesome sore. It should be taken in hand promptly, when first discovered. The bird affected with canker ought not to be permitted to remain an hour in the same pen or run with well fowls. It will go from one bird to another with wonderful celerity, and the fancier who finds it fairly started in his flock should immediately remove the sick fowl to a place by itself. Upon old hens or upon game cocks after they have been fought or "exercised," if it breaks out, it is very hard to cure. Unless the fowl be a really valuable one, the process is so slow in removing it that it hardly pays for the trouble it causes. Upon games old cockers

use saline washes and alum water, frequently bathing and cleansing the disordered parts, ofttimes with success at last. An alternate washing of burnt alum dissolved in new rum and chlorate of potash in a rum solution is excellent. The sore places should be cleansed thoroughly every morning and evening, and the canker removed daily. If taken in its very earliest stages, the canker spots may be advantageously touched with a weak solution of nitrate of silver. This will burn off the sores if followed up before they get too soft and pulpy.

Another remedy is to first remove all cankerous matter possible. Wash out the mouth and throat with water, then apply with a soft brush equal parts tincture of myrrh, borax and chlorate of potash till the sore looks clean, then dust with powdered borax till healed. In some cases ordinary Dalmatian insect powder, when slightly sprinkled on the roof of the mouths,(only a pinch being used) has proved beneficial.

THE GAPES.

Gapes are caused by a collection of small thread-like worms in the the wind pipe of the chicken. To kill these worms and not hurt the chicken is the requirement. Coal oil of the cheaper grades is a more effectual insecticide than the refined. Dr. Elzey's method is to take a small glass tube with a small rubber bulk, which apothecaries sell for a "medicine dropper," half fill it with coal oil, and inserting the tip into the windpipe, discharge the oil. The gapes are cured. A small oil can used for sewing machines will do in place of the medicine dropper. Operate as follows: Place the chicken back down, between your knees, and hold him gently; open his bill and draw the tongue out. Seize the lower mandible and tongue thus drawn out between the forefinger and thumb nail of the left hand. This will bring into view the opening of the windpipe at the base of the tongue, into which gently insert the tube and discharge the oil. Close the bill, and hold the head still for a few seconds. Then let the chicken go and he will cough, spattering some of the oil out, but enough remains to destroy the worms and they will be coughed up and swallowed. The gapes continue for a time after the treatment, but the remedy will be effectual in every case if properly applied, and it may readily be repeated, if thought worth while, as often as necessary. After a little practice it is easily applied and always succeeds.

The easiest treatment, according to "Poultry Diseases," is to put some carbolic acid of the clear, transparent quality into a spoon or metal saucer and hold it over a lamp. Dense, white fumes will arise. Hold the chicken's head in these until it is nearly suffocated. Or, shut all the affected chickens into a box and fumigate them together, but watch then closely lest they be killed. Burned sulphur fumes will also do very well for this purpose. The vapor of spirits of turpentine and of creosote are also recommended. Another method is to take a feather, which has been stripped of all the webbed portion save its tip, and dip it into spirits of turpentine or kerosene and thrust it into the windpipe and turn it around several times. Some of the worms will be killed, some will come out with the feather, some will be coughed out at once; catch on a sheet of paper and burn them all. The opening of the wind pipe is easily found at the base of the tongue.

As the subject is very important, we add still other methods of treatment recommended. Camphor has been given in pills the size of a pea, with success. Alum and sulphur in the form of fine powder, blown down the throat, will destroy the worms. Lime in the air will also effect the purpose, and may be applied by putting the chickens into a box covered with fine muslin and sifting fine lime through this, but not so fast as to smother the chicken. Another method, by some deemed doubtful and dangerous, is to pinch the chickens throat; this will crush the worms and cause them to loosen their hold, when they will be coughed up.

It has been discovered that *fresh* insect powder, blown into the mouth or windpipe, is excellent. Keep the chicks on new and clean ground, or on boards, and dust air-slaked lime freely over their runs.

CHOLERA.

This name is given to a disorder of obscure origin and character, which has proved itself to be one of the most rapidly destructive known to poultry keepers. Anything that tends to lower the constitutional vigor of the fowl will render it liable to an excess of this disease. Unwholesome food, given at irregular periods, impure and stagnant water as a drink, exposure to the weather or to the depressing heat of the sun without shade, all of these causes, so readily enumerated, increase the liability of the fowl to this disorder, as well as to many others. Among the causes most prominent in fostering the disease is, it is agreed on all hands, an over-crowded condition of the coops. In the first place such a condition of things is directly depressing to the fowls; in the second place the bad air makes good soil for the development of poisonous "germs," if any such there be. Cholera has been known, however, to attack flocks that are not kept in houses at all. Such cases can be explained by the fact that fowls thus kept are generally badly protected from the weather, and beside this, they really crowd together at their roosting places, which are sure to be tainted by an accumulation of droppings. Cholera seems also to be more prevalent in very hot and in very dry seasons.

It is thought to be infectious, but the infection does not seem to travel very far. Fowls roosting near fowls sick with cholera will catch it, but whether from them or from their droppings does not appear. This is the gist of the grounds of the statement that the specific poison which produces cholera is generated locally on premises where the disease exists, though it may be carried by pigeons, or birds from other yards.

Lesions.—The organ most changed is the liver. This is found enlarged, dark green, full of dark blood, congested and usually tender; it can easily be crushed in the hand. The gizzard is softer and sometimes much smaller than natural, and contains half-digested food. The crop and intestines are often full of sour, fermenting food, and ulcerated, and the intestines are much inflamed and "sore," that is, excoriated. The testicles have been found much altered. The condition of the liver now is the main thing to be noted. Of course, you will find the brain, nerves and lungs more or less congested, full of darker blood than usual, and the heart perhaps enlarged. The blood is darker and thicker than usual, and this condition, together with that of the liver, are thought by Dr. Dickie to exist in no other disease. The liver is not only the organ most altered, but apparently it is the one attacked first.

Symptoms and Diagnosis.—The disease must be made out before death, rather from its sudden epidemic character than anything else. It comes *suddenly in some cases; a fowl well to-day may be dead to-morrow*, and a whole flock may be thus rapidly carried off. In fact, it kills within 36 hours. The discharges are thought by some authorities to be decisive. These are mild at first, are yellowish green, or like sulphur and water, becoming thinner, greener, and more frothy as the disease goes on, and never stopping until the fowl is dead. The breathing becomes heavy and fast, the crop fills with mucous and wind; at last the food is not digested, the eyes close, and in a few hours the fowl dies." There is weakness, sometimes extreme, at the commencement of the disease; the fowl may even be unable to stand well. It does not plume itself, and has a general sleepy, moping appearance. At the later period, the dark, thickened blood may turn the comb and wattles dark, or may readily flow through them, so they become pale. There is much fever, great thirst, and a rapid, weak pulse. Cramps may occur. The fowl may die from the digestive disturbances, or apparently from paralysis of the heart or lungs, caused by the poisoned blood. Intense thirst is a symptom which is a sure indication.

Treatment.—You cannot save the lives of all of those attacked, neither will the same treatment that is good in the North succeed in the South. *Remove your whole flock at once to clean quarters*, if possible to some gravelly site that has never been used before for stock, and see that they are healthily housed there, and in all regards in a healthful condition. *Separate the sick from the well*, and if it were possible it would be well to to have every hen, *especially every sick hen*, have a place apart. This is practicable enough with some valuable pets.

The following is a treatment of the disease: As the birds will not eat, add a teaspoonful of liquid carbolic acid to each gallon of the drinking water. The remedy is heroic, but there is no sure cure. Do not mistake cholera for indigestion.

Remember that cholera *kills quickly*, and the birds always have intense thirst.

Diarrhœa.—How should fowls affected with diarrhœa be treated?

Too much feed may cause it, and it is often mistaken for cholera. When birds are very fat, fed on grain exclusively, do not have a variety, or lack grit, the result will be diarrhœa. The remedy is to withhold all feed for 48 hours, and then allow, for a few days, a pound of lean meat, cooked, to 20 birds, once a day. Add 20 drops tincture of nux vomica to each quart of drinking water, which avoids handling. A gill of linseed-meal, in soft feed for six hens, may be given once a day, for two or three days, after they improve. Diarrhœa in chicks occurs mostly from lack of warmth, hence plenty of warmth is essential. Give cooked feed, and add ten drops tincture nux vomica to each quart of their drinking water. Roup always attacks chicks in the bowels, hence if they die off, as if by a contagious diarrhœa, there is no remedy, though warmth may save some.

Discharge at Nostrils.—Is a discharge at the nostrils a sure indication of roup?

It indicates a cold, usually from a top draught of air from some source, and may lead to roup.

Indigestion.—Give remedies for indigestion in fowls.

Indigestion may produce either constipation, by causing inflammation, or diarrhœa or dysentery. It may be accompanied by a fever or loss of appetite, and apparently pain in the stomach. The crop is sometimes swollen, and the liver may become seriously affected. It is sometimes due to cold but is generally due to too much or too stimulating diet. Cut down the diet to a little meat and bone, and give grass or green food. (See Diarrhœa.)

Leg Weakness.—My hens seem unable to move about on their legs. What ails them?

It is usually the results of a fat condition of the hens and the heavy weight of the male, his attentions causing injury to the spine. The remedy is to remove the male. Fowls, especially cockerels that grow too fast, squat down on the ground.

Sometimes there is also a deficiency of earthy matter in the bones. Bone dust may be freely used. Feed with substances which do not tend to fat; wheat barley, meat. Internally may be given iron, three to eight grains of the citrate daily, or some form of iron and quinine. Hinton's recipe is sulphate of iron one grain a day; strychnine one sixteenth of a grain, phosphate of lime five grains, sulphate of quinine half a grain; thrice daily.

Rheumatism.—What is the cause of and cure for rheumatism?

Rheumatism generally comes from exposure to cold and wet, as by running in the wet grass in the morning, wet roosting places, etc., though most frequently from feeding sulphur in the feed, especially during damp weather. The malady is also hereditary. The symptoms are leg weakness, stiff joints, or contraction of the toes. The treatment consists mainly in warm, dry quarters and good stimulating feed; a little cooked meat every day. Rub the legs well with hot mustard water, afterwards wiping quite dry. Half a grain of opium (a quarter of a grain for a chicken of three months), night and morning soothes the pain.

Cholera Symptoms.—What are the symptoms of chicken cholera, with cure?

Symptoms are intense thirst, debility, followed by prostration, with greenish droppings. Give a teaspoonful of carbolic acid in a gallon of water—no other drink.

Constipation.—I have had several cases of the hindquarters in chickens, both young and old protruding fully an inch. Will you please tell me the cause and give me the remedy?

Probably due to constipation. Give a tablespoonful of linseed oil meal once a day, in the feed, for six hens, and feed plenty of grass.

Skin Disease.—What is the matter with my chicks? The down comes off and leaves a scale on their heads. Have looked for lice.

It may be due to some cutaneous disease. Try anointing the head once a day with a mixture composed of ten drops of carbolic acid, one teaspoonful cedar oil and a teaspoonful sweet oil.

Dampness.—I have out of seventy-five chickens six or eight roosters—no pullets—with the extended crops, and they draw their heads down to their shoulders and act as though they were stiff. Their legs seem weak, and with difficulty they can get on low roosts.

It may be due to the large lice on the heads, or from dampness, but most probably the former. Anoint heads with a few drops of sweet oil.

Treatment for Lice.—How can I get rid of lice on my fowls?

First clean up the premises. Saturate kerosene oil over every part, especially on the under side of roosts. Dust fowls well with insect powder. Provide them a dust bath. Grease their heads and necks with warm lard. Repeat this twice or three times a week. It means hard work.

Roup or Indigestion.—I have a lot of chickens as large as quails. They act as though they were choked, open their mouths to breathe, make a noise like sneezing. Some have died. They eat well, have a free run, are fed corn meal wet with warm water and sour milk, and were growing nicely until taken with this trouble.

It may be due to exposure, especially during damp weather, followed by indigestion. Warm quarters and anointing their heads with a few drops of sweet oil, will answer.

Scabby Legs.—Please give a remedy for scabby legs!

Mix a teaspoonful of kerosene and a gill of lard and a little sulphur. Apply on the legs once a week, the mixture to be warm. Wash occasionally with soap.

Swollen Crop.—What is the cause and cure of swollen crop?

If the crop is soft and puffy it is known as "sour crop" and if swollen and feverish is difficult to cure; if hard the passage to the gizzard is probably obstructed. Taken in time, either case is easily remedied, but at times it may be a case requiring an incision to remove the contents. It is usually caused by some substance obstructing the outlet from the crop to the gizzard.

Colds.—Please state what is the matter with cockerels or chickens when they make a noise at night while on their roost when drawing breath like a person does when he is gargling his throat.

It is due to a heavy cold, probably caused by a top draught in poultry house. Sprinkle a pinch of chlorate of potash down the throat once a day. Add a teaspoonful of permangenate of potash to each gallon of the drinking water. Keep them warm and free from draughts.

Trouble with Oviduct.—What treatment should be given for inflammation of the oviduct? What causes it?

It results from taking cold or unwholesome feed or feed that is over stimulating. The symptoms are general feverishness, feathers puffed out, continual straining on the part of the hen, imperfect eggs, etc. Remove hen from the cock and keep her on straw. Give no feed except a teaspoonful of linseed meal, daily, for a week.

Apoplexy.—I have lost some chickens that acted as though they had a spasm. On examining them found the skin had turned a dark red. They were taken suddenly, and tried to stand on their heads. I feed a warm feed in the morning, oats at noon, corn at night. What is it?

This was probably apoplexy—a sudden rush of blood to the head, and a rupture of a blood vessel there. The remedy is *prevention*. You have probably been overfeeding, and should give only two meals per day. Reduce the grain feed and give steamed clover or some such bulky feed instead. Above all *make them work* for their food by obliging them to scratch it up. Exercise is one of the best preventives of disease.

Worms.—What shall I give for internal worms?

Give a half teaspoonful of sulphur in food. Worm-seed, a tablespoonful to six hens three times a week, may be also given.

Pip.—Please tell me the easiest and best way to take "pip" off hens' tongues. Is the "pip" injurious to the hens?

"Pip" is simply a dryness of the tongue, caused by the bird breathing through the open mouth. It is not a disease nor is it dangerous.

Sulphur.—Would it be good policy to mix powdered sulphur with the food for fowls?

There is sulphur in the eggs, so it is safe to presume that sulphur in their feed would not be advantageous.

Symptoms of Rheumatism.—I am puzzled to know what is the matter of chickens that lose all strength in their feet and legs ; the toes seem to cramp up, and they are unable to stand.

This is probably rheumatism, which affects chicks and fowls just as it does human beings, and is due to acid in the blood, or is an aciduous condition of the blood. Rub the feet and legs with a good strong liniment, and feed warming, stimulating feed; give them milk to drink.

Red Mites.—How shall I proceed to get the hen house free of red mites?

The red vermin is the red spider, louse or red mite. Kerosene kills them at once, and as their haunts are the cracks and crevices of the roosting poles, and the sides of the buildings, nest boxes, etc., they are easy to destroy. If they are numerous go over the whole inside of the building with hot whitewash, sopping it on freely, so every crack and crevice is filled. Clean out and whitewash nest boxes, clean up the floor and put in fresh sand, and start all fresh and clean.

White Comb.—What makes the combs of some of my fowls turn white, and what is the treatment?

A pale light comb indicates that the bird is not well. A healthy bird has a red comb. When the bird is sick the pale comb appears, and changes to black when the bird is extremely ill.

Catarrh and Bronchitis.—Please describe catarrh and bronchitis.

The general symptoms of catarrh are a watery discharge from the eyes and nostrils. Catarrh is identical in appearance with the first stages of the roup. If it extends to the air tubes, then it is called bronchitis, and one of the symptoms is the symptoms is the coughing of the fowl. As soon as the watery discharge at the nostrils is discovered, the fowl should be taken to a dry, warm room and fed sparingly on soft feed either warm or lukewarm, and aconite should be mixed with the drinking water in the proportion of eight drops of the tincture to a pint of water. If the discharge at the beak becomes of a putrid and offensive character, you may consider that the fowl has the roup. In all cases of catarrh look out for the roup.

A Fall Tonic.—Will you name a good tonic for moulting hens?

The moulting hens will be greatly relieved and assisted in feathering if given some kind of tonic, and one of the best is to mix together 20 grains of quinine, 20 grains of chloride of iron, 40 grains of red pepper, one pound of boneset, one ounce of sulphur, and half a pound of salt. Put a teaspoonful of the mixture in some kind of soft food, for every six hens, three times a week. Give meat occasionally, and feed mixed grains. Moulting fowls take cold very easily should the weather change suddenly, and care must be taken to keep them warm and dry.

Another good tonic is tincture of perchloride of iron, 2 drachms; compound tincture of gentian, 2 drachms; lime water, 2 ounces; eggs beaten, 2 ounces; cod liver oil, 4 ounces. Shake thoroughly up into an emulsion, and give two tablespoonfuls three times a day. In scrofulous tendency or hereditary weakness the above is an excellent stock medicine, and may be given to young chicks in ten-drop doses mixed with the feed. It is often valuable in diarrhœa, and also during molt.

Frosted Comb.—Is there a cure for frosted combs?

A cure for frosted or frozen combs and wattles is equal parts of turpentine and sweet oil applied twice daily as soon as discovered. Glycerine is also good. Protect the bird from cold draughts or winds.

Insects in Brooder.—May I ask you how to remove the insects from my chicks, three days old, now in a brooder, hatched by hens?

Dust them with *fresh* insect powder every day, and rub the brooder with kerosene oil. Smear a few drops of warm lard on the heads and necks of the chicks twice a week.

Large Lice.—What is wrong with fowls when they stand with heads thrown back on shoulders, and legs weak?

A reply to the above is that there is a probability that your fowls have the large lice on the skin of the head and necks. Anoint with a few drops of sweet oil on heads, necks and vents.

Warts.—Can you tell me what will cure warts on chickens? We have a pullet that has eight on her face, two of which are on her eye. They are growing rapidly and we fear will close the eye entirely. What causes it?

It may be the effects of chicken pox, or the work of minute parasite. Such cases happen as the after results of roup, sometimes. Try an ointment, apply daily for a week, of ten parts sweet oil, one part spirits turpentine, one of cedar oil, and half part carbolic acid.

Sore Head.—What is a good remedy for sore heads in fowls?

Epsom salts is the best remedy for sore head. Salts will cure all ordinary cases, and will certainly prevent this disagreeable disease spreading in flock. Put it in soft feed or put in drinking water. A tablespoonful to a gallon of dough or a gallon of drinking water is the proportion. Continue its use every other day until disease is eradicated from the flock. In addition to salts in the water, take equal parts pulverized table salt, bluestone and lard, or axle grease, adding a teaspoonful of carbolic acid to each half pint, well mixed, and grease the head and face of the fowls or chicks that are affected.

Disinfectant.—Give a recipe for a cheap but effective disinfectant.

A cheap and good disinfectant to use about poultry houses and yards when contagious fowl diseases are present or feared, is made by dissolving three pounds of copperas in five gallons of water, and adding one pint of crude carbolic acid. Sprinkle about the house and yard with a common watering pot.

Bromide of Potash.—How should bromide of potash be administered to fowls?

Bromide of potash is recommended for roup and brain disorders. Give 5 to 7 grains a day to each sick fowl, also gargle the throats with kerosene oil, inject a few drops into the nostrils. As a preventive of roup, give two grains to each fowl in their drinking water.

Scouring.—Have a game pullet that has not laid for a month. Her droppings are very soft, like white of an egg, and stay around the vent. Her comb is beginning to shrink, she will drink a little, but not eat much. Could find no lice.

The pullet is probably scouring, caused perhaps, by too much soft feed certainly by improper diet. (See Diarrhœa.)

Boil on Foot..—Please inform me how to cure a boil on top of the foot of a hen. It extends under her foot also. She can scarcely walk.

It may be bumble foot, due to high roost. If soft, lance it and wash once a day with a solution of twenty drops carbolic acid in a gill of warm water. Keep it bound up with a soft rag saturated with warm mutton suet.

Condition Powders.—Will you give a formula for a good condition powder?

Carbonate of iron 1 oz; anise seed, 2 oz; powdered ginger, 6 oz; mustard, 1 oz; table salt, 2 oz; sulphur, 2 oz; licorice, 4 oz; powdered charcoal, 14 oz. These, powdered and mixed thoroughly make two pounds of good condition powders, and if kept in a tight box will be serviceable for a long time. A teaspoonful in ten quarts of soft feed, or in that proportion, fed every day in warm weather, or every other day in stormy and cold weather, will prove of great service. For growing chicks, one-half the amount of powders in the same quantity of feed is sufficient. A teaspoonful of the tincture of iron to each gallon of drinking water should be provided in all bad seasons.

Fumigation.—State the best plan of fumigation.

Take a small furnace, or stove pot, or an iron kettle, into which place a pound or two of crude roll sulphur, broken up. Close the doors and windows (during the absence of the fowls in the forenoon), and set the contents of the vessel on fire in the centre of the floor. Shut the house up tight and leave it to smoke a couple of hours. This will finish the vermin completely, for the time being. Then open all the windows and doors for subsequent thorough ventilation, and your fowls will realize the benefit of this cleansing for weeks afterward.

Enteritis.—Having some fowls affected with inflammation of the bowels, or enteritis would like to know its cause.

Enteritis, or inflammation of the bowels, is a common disorder among poultry. It has so many symptoms in common with chicken cholera, is so rapid in its course, that many pronounce it real cholera. Acute, chronic, dysenteric and membraneous enteritis are the most common forms. Acute enteritis is a disease that often attacks fowls occupying confined runs and uncleanly kept houses, or those fed on damaged grains, decomposed meat, or sour meal and irritating seeds or plants. It is occasionally caused by surfeiting the fowls with improper food, indigestion, the rupture of an ovum and its escape into the abdominal cavity, sharp splinters of bone piercing some of the intestines, etc. The first period of the disease often passes unnoticed, especially where the poultry does not receive the closest attention. However, the first day the bird is dejected, loses its naturally healthy and cheerful appearance, and is without appetite. The second day the crop is found empty, the beak slightly opened, the mucus membrane of the mouth dry, the pulse quick and irregular, and the skin hot. From this time the symptoms become intensified as the disease progresses. A diarrhœa is noticed from the first—the matter passed at first being nearly solid, then becoming semi-liquid and finally very thin; serous, of a whitish, greyish, yellowish color, and a disagreeable odor. The course of the disease does not extend over three or four days, and unless its severity is mitigated, either by natural causes or proper treatment, the bird at this time indicates extreme suffering by agitating its wings, stretching its neck and frequently opening its mouth—death soon following.

Egg Bound.—What are the symptoms and treatment of this difficulty?

The hen comes off the nest without laying and walks about distressed, hanging down her wings. Sometimes she remains on the nest. Give teaspoonful of castor oil, if this is unsuccessful, wash the vent well with warm water and then pass in an oiled feather, or better, inject an ounce of sweet oil. The egg is too large. Eggs have been known to accumulate and form a large tumor. It affects mostly hens that are highly fed.

Canker.—My hens have some kind of a disease. They choke, their mouths are filled with hard matter, and if you take it off it will bleed. Their eyes emit matter.

They have canker. With a soft rag, on a stick, swab the mouths with a solution made by dissolving a piece of blue vitriol, as large as a chestnut, in a gill of water. Inject a few drops of kerosene in each nostril. (See Canker.)

Water Crop.—How is water crop described and how treated?

The symptom of a bird with water crop is a poor appetite, but it craves and drinks water until its crop is distended and becomes sour. To treat, take a bowl of water in which dissolve a quarter of a teaspoonful of baking soda, and take the fowl's head in the left hand and with the body under the arm, holding head downward, with the neck distended, hold the beak open with the right hand and manipulate the contents of the crop down and out of the mouth. Then give a good dose of soda water; a spoonful is sufficient. Manipulate as before, rinsing out the crop well and being careful not to irritate the crop so as to cause inflammation Coop the chick by itself, feed sparingly a few day days with bread and scraps from the table, with a sprinkling of charcoal. This will generally cure it.

Swelled Heads and Sore Eyes.—Have a fowl that has swelled head and sore eyes, but does not appear to have roup. What about her?

It is due to a draught of air on her at night. The eye next the draught becomes affected first. Often the head is swollen and great lumps appear, in which stage the disease has become roup. Mix one part of spirits of turpentine and four parts sweet oil. Anoint head. face and comb once a day.

Liver Disease.—Three of my hens died. One seemed perfectly healthy, was laying nearly every day, had a red comb, and I

could see nothing the matter with it. The liver of another was five times as large as it should be, and the other had been ailing quite a while, but would always eat. The liver of this one had hard white spots as large as a quarter dollar on it. Is it cholera or liver complaint?

Should say the last was liver disease, second enlargement of the liver, (or fatty degeneration of liver), and the first apoplexy. Fowls not infrequently drop dead of this trouble. It is caused by condition powders, copperas solution, Douglass mixture, and overfeeding on stimulating food. Give your fowls no drugs. They cause disease.

Lack of Grit.—I had several pullets sick and one died. Their crops were full of feed, and quite hard. I feed soft feed in the morning, and grain at noon and night. What is in their crops had been there several days. What was it?

This is probably want of grit and overfeeding. The want of grit in the crop and gizzard is to a fowl what lack of teeth would be to us. A toothless person *could* be fed on soups, etc., and life sustained; but 'twould be a profitless existence. What would biddy do when she has nothing with which to grind up the feed in the gizzard? She simply starves to death. Lack of grit and drugs are most fruitful causes of fowl ills that we have to treat.

GENERAL SUGGESTIONS.

When your hens get sore feet, or have bumble foot, it means that your roosts are too high.

Always have your nests removable, and kerosene the roosts, (under and upper sides) once a week.

Feed no sulphur as it will cause rheumatism, or leg weakness. Never give it in damp weather.

Giving water to chicks so as to allow them to get their bodies wet is certain death, as dampness is fatal to them.

A mixture of two parts lard and one of sulphur and kerosene oil will remove the rough, scabby formation on the legs of fowls.

Do not waste time trying to cure egg bound hens, or persistent cases of roup. The labor will be worth more than the hens.

Don't be too anxious for ventilation in winter. You will have more difficulty keeping the cold air *out* than to let it *in*. Fowls dislike winds and draughts.

Disinfect the entire premises, when disease appears, with Douglass' Mixture, which is made of two gallons water, one pound copperas, and one gill sulphuric acid.

For warts, sorehead and skin diseases, rub once a day with a few drops of the following: Lard, two tablespoonfuls; cedar oil, one teaspoonful; carbolic acid, twenty drops.

When you find a dead hen under the roost the cause is apoplexy, from overfeeding. When your hens gradually droop and die remove the cock, as he is the cause, especially if he is heavy. If a hen has the blind staggers she is too fat.

If your hens "pip,"[or have swelled heads or eyes, there is a crack or hole in the wall. Usually the draughts from some ventilator are the cause, and the surest remedy is to keep the house closed at night, but it must be kept clean.

When your birds have swelled heads or eyes, or a hoarse breathing, ten chances to one you have a crack or crevice in your poultry house, or draughts come in from the *top* ventilator. The top ventilator has killed thousands of valuable fowls.

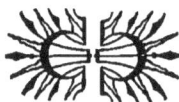

CHAPTER III.

About Eggs.

Soft-Shelled Eggs.—My hens have plenty of lime in the shape of plastering and oyster shells, but they lay soft-shelled eggs. Why?

Soft shelled eggs are due to some cause not known. There is no remedy for it. Fowls which occasionally have this fault will come around all right in time. Do not doctor them for it.

Dark and White in Color.—Which breeds of fowls lay dark colored eggs? Which lay white?

Either of the following breeds will be found to lay dark, viz: Cochins, Brahmas, Wyandottes, Plymouth Rocks or Langshans. Where eggs with white shells are wished, they will be produced by Leghorns, Minorcas, Andalusians, Polish, Hamburgs, Games, Houdans or Dorkings. Where both are required, Plymouth Rocks or Wyandottes, with the Leghorn or Minorcas, will be found to fill the demand most satisfactorily.

How Prolific.—Please let me know how many eggs Leghorns, Black Spanish, Minorcas, Hamburgs, Light Brahmas, Plymouth Rocks and Wyandottes lay in a year on an average?

The Leghorns, Black Spanish, Minorcas and Hamburgs are usually credited with about 200 apiece a year; Light Brahmas about 100 to 125; The Plymouth Rocks and Wyandottes about 150. About 100 eggs a year for each hen in a flock, is considered an average.

Brown Eggs.—Do all pure Light Brahmas lay a dark brown egg? Out of my flock of fifteen a few lay dark brown eggs, the others very light brown. What other breeds are there that lay dark brown eggs? Do any of the Plymouth Rocks lay them?

Brahmas and Cochins lay brown or dark eggs. The Plymouth Rocks, Langshans and Wyandottes lay eggs that are somewhat dark, though many of them produce light ones. It is seldom that the eggs of a flock are uniform of the breeds mentioned.

Greater Production.—Can egg production be increased?

Yes, by feeding clover and meat instead of grain exclusively, and keeping the hens in exercise, so as to avoid having them too fat.

How Much Cold.—How many degrees of cold will eggs (that are being saved for hatching) stand, and not spoil them for hatching purposes?

They should not be exposed to lower than 40 degrees above zero. An egg freezes at about 10 degrees above zero, which kills the germ.

Small in Size,—What will cure a hen of laying eggs far too small for her size?

The trouble with such hens is that they are too old to be of any further use. Such eggs are sterile. When hens are young and do thus, the cause is generally high feeding, and a course of light diet will help the matter.

Testing for Incubator.—When should incubating eggs be tested and how?

Eggs ought to be tested when seven days old. This is done by holding them before a candle or strong light, and looking through them, the hand shading the light from the eyes. If clear, the egg is infertile, but is quite good for cooking. If it is dark in the centre, shading off to lighter at the edges, it is fertile. Two days before hatching they can again be tested, put in water heated to 105 degrees, or as hot as the hand can bear it. The eggs containing live chickens will be seen to jump about, while the dead eggs will either sink or float movelessly. This water test will soften the shell and assist hatching very materially.

Washing before Incubation.—Is it not a good plan to wash eggs that come from other yards before incubation?

Before eggs obtained from strange yards are placed under a hen, or into a hatching machine, they should be carefully washed with warm water, rinsed, and wiped quite dry. If this is carefully done there is not any possibility of injuring the eggs; on the contrary, they will be in better condition, as the pores of the shell have been freed from dirt. We believe that disease germs may be conveyed in the dirt attached to the shell of an egg. Do not wash the eggs until they are about to be placed in a machine or under a hen.

How to Pack in Jars.—Will you state a good method of packing eggs?

Slack a peck of clean lime, pour in six pails of water and drop in three quarts of salt. Stir until all is dis-olved; then let it settle and it is ready for use. Pack the eggs in jars, pour on the thinner lime water, cover the jar with a cloth, and over this spread a coating of the thicker portion of the lime. The jars must not be filled too full, as the water must never be allowed to get below the tops of the eggs. Each peck of lime will preserve more than a hundred dozen of eggs. A six gallon jar will hold twenty dozen if rightly packed. The expense is very little.

Classification.—How are eggs classified in the market?

The Boston Chamber of Commerce has decided to classify eggs as follows: Extras, firsts, seconds, thirds and known marks. Extras shall comprise the very best qualities fresh-laid, clean eggs in season. put up in the best manner, where every condition necessary to place fine eggs in Boston market has been complied with. Firsts shall comprise fine marks of eggs such as come in carload lots, or smaller lots, and are packed in fine order, fresh in season and reasonably clean, such stock as gives satisfaction to most customers. Seconds shall comprise all stock that is merchantable and inferior to firsts. Thirds shall comprise all poor stock in bad order, rotten, etc.; stock not considered really merchantable. Known marks shall comprise such sorts as are well known to the trade under some particular designation or mark, shall be of such quality as those familiar with the mark generally understand it to be, in the season in which it is

offered. Extras to pass at the mark must not lose to exceed one dozen per 100 dozen, and firsts not more than two dozen per 100 or one and a half dozen per barrel, if sold in barrels.

Egg Eaters.—My hens eat their eggs. What can I do to prevent it?

Make nests in a dark place and have them ten inches off the floor, with tops, so that hens must enter them from the front. As the hens cannot reach the eggs from the floor, and cannot well stand up in the nests, they will soon be cured of the vice.

Packing for Shipment.—What is the best method of packing eggs for shipment?

In packing eggs it is now universally the custom to wrap each egg in paper; this is an essential precaution. But in regard to the material used for filling in between the eggs, many sorts are used, but all are not good. Of the sorts in general use, the chaff from a hay mow is the least objectionable, as eggs packed in it frequently go long distances and hatch well. But in our estimation the very best material for packing, and one well adapted to come into general use, is oats, the basket to be covered with excelsior held in place by sewing cheese cloth around it. Where cheese cloth is used, the most customary way of fastening it is by using a carpet needle and cotton twine, sewing it down with a few long stitches, through the interstices of the splints, and packing the excelsior between the cloth and basket.

Dry Packing—Is dry packing as safe as moist packing for eggs?

Dry packing for eggs is as safe as wet packing and much more convenient, but eggs must be kept from the air and turned twice per week or they will adhere to the shell. Pack in small boxes with light covers so they may be turned over without handling the eggs. Use dry salt, dust, plaster, fine ashes or meal, and keep in a cool place, 40 to 60 degrees. By this means strictly fresh eggs may be kept from two to six months and frequently one, by holding them three months, will find a rise of five to 12 cents per dozen. Infertile eggs keep better than fertile ones. To sell eggs at

13 to 16 cents, as many do, is folly, and although preserved eggs do not look as well nor bring quite the price of fresh ones, they may be depended on and the process pays one well for his labor.

Bloody Spots.—I frequently find a fresh drop of blood in eggs. Please state the cause.

It is due to the rupture of a minute blood vessel during the formation of the eggs, especially when hens are very highly fed. It is not a serious matter.

Fertilization.—How soon are eggs fertilized after a male is admitted to flock?

Usually about five days, but much depends upon circumstances, such as position of the eggs, etc.

Selecting for Incubation.—Is there any rule to guide in choosing eggs for hatching?

In selecting eggs for hatching select those that are of good shape, and uniform in size. If one or two of the lot are small, the chicks will be correspondingly small, and as a general thing, weak. Choose eggs from strong, vigorous fowls, that have been bred with some end in view.

Preserving Process.—I would like a good recipe for preserving eggs.

The following is known as the Havana process: Take 24 gallons of water, 12 lbs. of unslaked lime, and 4 lbs. of salt, or in that proportion according to the quantity of eggs to be preserved; stir it well several times a day, and then let it stand till the liquor has settled and is perfectly clear. Draw or carefully dip off the clear liquid, leaving the sediment at the bottom. Take for the above amount of liquid 5 ounces each of baking soda, cream of tartar, saltpetre and borax and an ounce of alum. Pulverize and mix these, and dissolve in one gallon of boiling water, and add to the mixture about 20 gallons of pure lime water. This will about fill a cider barrel. Put the eggs in carefully, so as not to crack any of the shells, letting the water always stand an inch above the eggs, which can be done by placing a barrel head a little smaller upon them and weighting it. This amount of liquid will preserve 150 dozen eggs. It is not necessary to wait to get a full barrel or smaller package of eggs, but they can be put in at any time that they can be obtained fresh. But the same liquid should be used only once.

Should Eggs Rest.—Does it injure eggs to ship them long distances, and how long should they rest before being put in incubators?

There is a foolish notion prevailing among some fowl breeders, that eggs which have been shipped a distance should rest a day or two before being placed in an incubator. As soon as the hens are ready to set, or the incubator ready for work, place the eggs under or in at once; they will rest as comfortably in either place as elsewhere, in fact, better; for everybody knows that the fresher the eggs the more chicks they will yield, and the healthier the chicks. The germ floats to the top of the egg and will find its way there in a half minute, at the most, if revolved a hundred time an hours; and the yolk will find its place just as soon if it has not been broken, in which case it might rest a month or a year and never hatch. We have tried numerous eggs, travelling from 80 to 3,500 miles, and always found that the sooner incubation was started the better the result.

POINTERS ON PRESERVING EGGS.

1. Only *strictly fresh* eggs can be preserved, and in packing them the eggs should not touch each other, as one bad egg will spoil the whole.

2. Eggs collected from neighbors, or at stores, will not answer, as even the most obliging neighbor may unintentionally impose a stale egg on you.

3. Eggs from hens not in company with cocks will keep three times as long as will those from hens mated with cocks. Hence, in summer, after hatching is over, remove the males, as the hens will lay fully as well without them.

4. Keep the eggs as near sixty degrees as possible, but seventy is not too high. In other words, keep them in a *cool* place in summer, and do not let them freeze in winter. The cooler you keep them the better.

5. Eggs will keep in a *cool place*, if simply turned often, without any packing at all, especially if they are from hens not in company with cocks.

CHAPTER IV.

Poultry Buildings.

A BUILDING COSTING ABOUT $80.

[From our "Low Cost Poultry Houses."]

The building shown at Fig. 1 of the engraving on next page is 40 ft. front by 12 ft. in width, and same plans can be adapted to a lean-to structure if preferred. The arrangement of interior is simple. An alley 2 ft. 6 in. wide extends full length of building (see Fig. 4) with a cross alley 4 ft. wide from which entrance is had to the pens. Each pen is about 9 ft. square. The nests are so arranged as to be accessible for gathering the eggs from the long alley. At Fig. 2 a section of nest boxes and roosting perches is shown. The nests are one foot square with an opening to each box in alley-way. The location of the roosting perches and drop boards may be seen at Fig. 3. The perches are on a hinged frame so that they may be turned up out of the way when drop board is cleaned.

The house is sided with boards. The windows are 3x5 ft. 2 in. Partitions are boarded up 2 ft. from ground and above the boards there is 4 ft. wire netting. The inside doors are simply frames covered with wire. The following shows

COST OF MATERIAL.

1,300 sq. ft. matched boards, spruce	$26 00
350 ft. 2x4 joist	4 00
300 ft. 2x3 scantling	3 50
4 windows	20 00
250 sq. ft. wire netting	3 75
300 sq ft. tar roofing	6 00
Nails and hardware	1 00
Labor of carpenter	18 00
Total cost	$82 25

Each additional running foot front will cost approximately about $2.25.

Chaff, Straw, Etc.—I wish to put something on the floor of my hen house to throw feed on. In order to make the hens scratch for it. If chaff cannot be had will not shavings answer, having them three inches thick on the floor?

Yes," if broken fine; or you may use cut straw, which comes in bales.

Partitions.—Before I build my poultry house and yards, I would like to know, if I would have much trouble with my fowls fighting, if I should make the lower part of the partitions of wire netting?

Have the bottom of boards, two feet high, as they will peck each other through the wire.

Ventilation.—What is the best mode o ventilation?

The proper way to ventilate is to run a shaft 4x6 inches inside, from within 4 inches of the floor up through the roof and to a height of 2 feet above the highest point of the roof, putting on a cap to exclude rain, and snow, and leave side openings for a draught.

A Stone Walled House.—What would you think of building the walls of a poultry house of stone and mortar? I intend to build a house 15x100 feet, and as I am a stone mason by trade I can build it of stone for about half what the lumber would cost me.

Stone walls laid up in mortar and cement would make an excellent house, only that care should be taken to build it in midsummer, so that it would get thoroughly dry before frost comes. It would be greatly improved by fastening strips of furring to the inside, about three feet apart and then ceiling up. This would give an inch dead-air space to keep out dampness and frost, and make it much warmer than otherwise.

FIG. 1.

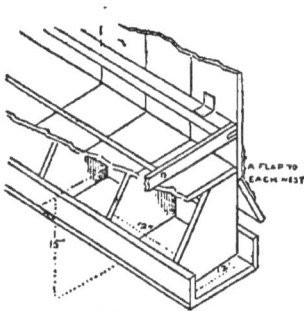

FIG. 2.

FIG. 3.

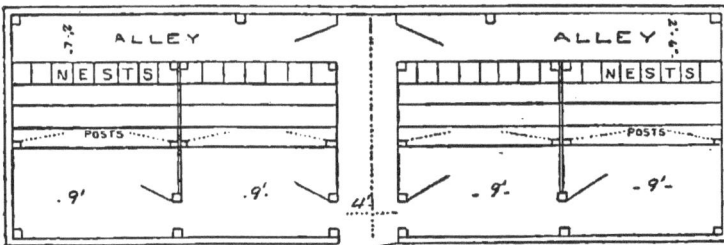

FIG. 4

A Poultry House Costing About $80.

Room in Winter.—How much floor space should 20 fowls have for a winter house?

A house 10x10 feet should accomodate 30 to 40 hens in the winter season without crowding, as they can, at this season, be together with less inconvenience, but the fact is the more room the better. It is not how much room on the roost is required, but how much room on the floor should be given, as that is where the hens are to work and scratch. If the hens have access to a covered shed in which to exercise during the day it will not matter, on cold nights, if 30 hens be allowed to roost in a house 10x10 feet, for they will get more fresh air than can be kept out, in the winter season. The rule of ten is a good one for calculating the space required, which is, in summer, to allow 10 hens in a house 6x10 feet, and allow them a yard 10x20 to 40 feet. In winter one-half that space will answer. The bigger the run the better.

Earth Floors.—What do you think about earth floors in poultry house?

Many prefer them. Use the most mellow soil you can procure. Loam is better than sand; the drier it is the better. If the air in your hennery is full of dust arising from the hens scratching and wallowing, then you may know that the premises are thoroughly disinfected. Especially is it beneficial to have an ample quantity of dry earth under the perches. The dust from fine, dry loam which settles upon the nest boxes, perches and every part of the woodwork tends to keep off vermin, so that in some cases no white-washing is necessary. Be sure by all means that the bed of earth which forms the floor is higher than the ground surrounding the building, so that the surface water, when there are thaws and rains will not run into the building. As an additonal precaution, surround the building with a shallow ditch communicating, if possible, with lower ground in the vicinity.

Chief Requirements—Being about to erect a poultry house, what are some of the chief requirements to be observed?

For economy's sake, the walls should not be carried up too high from the ground. The inside of a fowl house need not be over seven or eight feet high at the eaves, on either side, with a "one-third pitch"

above this for the roof. If the building has only a "shed" roof, or one slant of covering, the back wall may be three to five feet high, and the front seven or eight feet from the sills. In all cases look well to the means of having the building thoroughly ventilated, when desired. An opening in the ridge for this purpose, or one at both sides of the house under the eaves is best. Have a screen trap door or slide, inside, that may be raised or shut at will, conveniently. Nothing is more surely conducive to good health in your poultry, continuously, than affording them pure air to breathe. In confined premises where there is no opportunity for the rapidly accumulating foul air within to escape, chickens or adult birds cannot thrive. The breathing over and over of this impure atmosphere generates disease inevitably; and the careless or inexperienced breeder discovers "roup," "sniffles," swelled head," "pip," and a score of other so-called fowl diseases among his stock, most of which are fairly chargeable for their origin to this neglect regarding proper ventilation. Fresh air, clean water, varied feed, and all the range you can give the birds in good weather, are chief requirements toward their health and thrift. Of these, pure breathing may be counted as among the very first important requisites. Ventilation, however, must not permit of draughts, or come down on the fowls from the top.

House for Four Breeds.—Will you give directions for arranging a house for four different breeds? I do not want the building to be over 12x16 and it is to hold 20 of each breed.

The proper plan is to allow five square feet for each hen. That is, a house 5x10 feet (50 square feet), should accomodate 10 hens. You cannot arrange it to hold 80 birds, as you desire.

House and Yard.—How large a poultry house should I have to accommodate twenty-five laying hens? Would a yard 2 rods wide and 10 rods long do for that many hens? Would it keep them in grass if it was in an orchard? How high a netting fence should I have for pure Leghorns, or for a cross of Leghorns on Plymouth Rocks?

That number would do very well in a house 12x15 feet, and six feet high to eaves, but better in a house

13x20, divided into two pens 10x12, with yard divided in halves also. The size yard mentioned would be a liberal yard, and should keep in grass all the growing season. All the better if it is an orchard. A fence should be six feet for either kind; although with a liberal yard they are less likely to fly than if shut in a small yard.

Cement Floors.—Is cement floor good for poultry? If not, why?

It is better as a precaution against rats, but is cold, hence not so suitable as boards, and it is sometimes damp, owing to condensation of moisture. Put earth on it and it will be all right.

Heating a Poultry House.—What kind of heating apparatus would be best to heat a poultry house 32 feet long by 20 feet wide, hall in centre, cemented cellar 6 feet deep.

It is best to use no heating arrangement, as it may make the hens delicate and more liable to colds.

Leg Weakness from Board Floor.—Will keeping old chickens on board floors cause leg weakness if they have proper food? Can young chicks be rai ed to market age in a room with board floor?

Board floors will not cause leg weakness if the chicks are given litter to scratch in, and are given covering at night over them.

Ventilating a Cellar.—I have a cellar, 18 feet wide and 22 feet long, two windows at west end and one window at east end, with double doors. I want to keep 30 Leghorns in it this winter. How am I to ventilate it?

Do not ventilate at all in winter except to leave the doors open during the day. At night the house should be closed, no openings at all. It will be harder to keep out the cold air than you may think.

Various Questions.—How large a house for 100 hens? 2. Should laying room be partitioned off from roosting room? 3. 150 chickens in a house 10 feet square—are they too crowded? 4. How many roosters to 100 hens?

For permanent quarters, full grown fowls require at least five square feet of ground room per head. Thus 100 hens would need a house 10x50 feet—height is not so important. 2. Not necessarily. 3. Yes, or very soon will be, if they grow any. 4.

If for breeding, use one to a flock, of a dozen always. If for eggs only, and all in one flock, keep no male— two roosters in any flock is one to many.

South or Southeast.—In which direction should a poultry house face, to get the early sun's warmth? Some say south and some say southeast?

The southeast direction is proper if the warmth is desired very early, but there will be less warmth from the sun in the afternoon. We would advise the southeast direction for the reason that the morning is the time the warmth is most needed.

The Best Poultry House.—Which is the best plan for a poultry house?

A poultry house is like a dwelling house no two persons will agree. Much depends on climate, lay of the land, soil, etc. The most potent factor is the "pocket-book," as no matter what the plan may be, it must correspond with the contemplated cost. Hence, we can only reply that there is no best poultry house. Our book on "Low-cost Poultry Houses" (price 25 cents) has numerous plans with specifications and cost.

Winter Ventilation.—Is it necessary to ventilate in winter?

Ventilators to poultry houses have done more damage to poultry in winter than anything else. If the air of the poultry houses in winter is foul, some excuse may be made for the ventilator, but the severe cold seals up all sources of odor, and in a short time turns all liquids to solids. The poultry house can be amply purified and ventilated by leaving the doors and windows open during the day and using dry dirt on the roost board and floor as an absorbent, but the ventilator at the top of the poultry house should never be left open after cold weather sets in. Let your object in winter be to secure warmth first. Ventilation will take care of itself, and you will have more difficulty in keeping the cold air out than to let it in.

To Fumigate Poultry Houses.—Can you give some practical method of fumigating poultry buildings?

A writer in the Poultry World gives his method as follows: Turn out the fowls some cool or damp day, and close all the cracks in the house except the door. Then take a kettle of live coals and place on the ground in the centre, but if there is a wood floor lay a flat stone in on which to set the kettle. Throw a half-pound or pound of sulphur upon the coals and shut the door, and the house closed for a few hours, and we will venture to say no more lice or mites will be found in it for a few weeks thereafter. If the house is not tight enough to admit of a thorough fumigation in the manner described, then clean as well as you can, and then mix white-wash with fresh lime, mixing a liberal quantity of sulphur, after which throw sulphur into all the cracks, and apply kerosene oil to all the roosts. The house should be well aired before the fowls are admitted, and well ventilated at night. We have never known the "sulphur cure" to fail if properly applied.

ADDITIONAL QUESTIONS.

Is it positively necessary to have sunlight in poultry houses? (We should say yes.)—Should buildings always be ventilated? (Yes.)—Do you favor building near pig pens? (We do not.)—Should buildings be on a foundation above ground? (Yes, otherwise the surface water in heavy showers may make the floors wet and damp.)—Should perches be moveable? (By all means.)—What style of roof is most economical? (One with only one side which extends to the ground.)—Is wire preferable to lath for partitions? (We think so.)—Is a hall or passage way necessary? (It is decidedly preferable.)—Is a two-story building advantageous? (Yes; the roof costs no more and the upper story can be used for various purposes.—(What ought a good house for 60 or 80 fowls cost? (A good house with four pens can be built for $100 and perhaps less.)—How much room should a dozen fowls have? (About 12 feet square.)— What is a good cheap style of roof? (Roof boards of hemlock or spruce covered with tarred paper and then shingled.)—Where should the roosts be located? (Out of the line of draughts.)—What size should the roosting pole be? (A pole about the size of a person's wrist makes the best roosting pole and is better than 2x4 scantling.)—Are high roosts advisable? (Decidedly not.)—What should be the size of ventilators? (About five inches square inside measure and run below roost platforms.)—Should board floors be laid on or very near the ground? (They should be at least one foot above ground.)—What makes a good lining for a poultry house? (Tarred paper.)

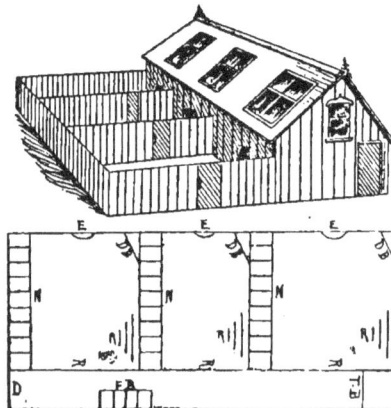

CHAPTER V.

Incubators and Broiler Raising

RULES FOR HATCHING WITH INCUBATORS.

1. Hatching chicks with an incubator is a winter pursuit.

2. The hen seldom sits in winter, hence she and the incubator do not conflict.

3. Eggs in winter do not hatch as well as eggs under hens in April.

4. Hens that lay in winter cannot produce as fertile eggs at that time as in the spring, for the cold season prevents exercise, the hens become fat and the pullets are not as fully matured, while the male, if he has a frosted comb, suffers from cold and becomes unserviceable.

5. Eggs are sometimes chilled in winter. When you buy them you take many chances.

6. Do not use extra large eggs, or small eggs. Have all eggs of normal size, and of perfect shape.

7. In winter the hen will not hatch one-half of her eggs nor raise one-third of her chicks.

8. Do not be afraid to watch your incubator. It pays as well to keep awake all night to watch a hundred chicks hatch out as it does to keep awake to save a $5 calf from loss when it is dropped and the chicks are worth more than the calf.

9. No incubator has brains. It will regulate but cannot think.

10. When chicks die in the shell the chances are that too much draught of air comes over them. When a hen is hatching she will fight if even a feather is lifted from her. She will allow not the slightest change of temperature and she will hatch as well in a dry place as in a moist location.

11. Dry warm nests in winter, and moist nests in summer, is an old proverb, hence the moisture depends on the season. Less is required in the incubator in winter.

12. Thermometers change. They should be tested frequently.

13. As the chicks progress in the eggs they give off heat, hence be careful of the lamp, hot water, or whatever the source of heat may be.

14. Too much moisture covers the egg and excludes the air from the chicks within the eggs.

15. No currents of air can pass through an incubator without a plentiful supply of moisture, but in incubators that have no currents but little moisture is needed.

16. Do not labor under the delusion that a young chick is always dying in the shell for lack of fresh air, and that it must have as much as a young animal.

17. Do not take out the chicks until you believe all are hatched. Leave the chicks in the incubator. If you take them out, the heat will suddenly drop, and you will also let in the cold air on the eggs. Never disturb the eggs when chicks are hatching.

18. Test your incubator with moisture, no moisture, plenty of air, and air shut off, as each incubator differs from the other.

19. Eggs will be aired sufficiently when the eggs are turned. It is of no consequence to cool them, but this depends on circumstances.

20. If chicks do not hatch out by the twenty-first day your heat is too low.

21. If the chicks begin to hatch on the eighteenth day your heat is rather high.

22. Do not put eggs in at different periods during the hatch, and do not hatch ducklings and chicks together.

23. The same rules apply to the eggs of hens, ducks, turkeys and guineas, as regards heat and moisture.

24. Never sprinkle eggs. It lowers the heat instantly, and sometimes kills the chicks in the shells.

25. If the incubator shows moisture on the glass, do not open the egg drawer until it is dry. Cold air and dampness kill the chick, the heat being lowered by rapid evaporation.

26. The reason why the hen that steals her nest hatches so well is because you do not give her all sorts of eggs, such as large eggs, small eggs and eggs from old hens and immature pullets, such a you put the in incubator.

27. Keep away the curious visitor just when your eggs are hatching.

28. Keep the incubator in a place of moderate temperature. A window on one side will make that side cooler than the other.

29. Let the bulb of the thermometer touch a fertile egg.

30. Begin with a 100-egg incubator, and learn, before you try a larger one.

31. No matter how much you read, experience will be the best teacher.

32. Have your incubator warm before you put in the eggs.

33. A child cannot manage an incubator, all claims to the contrary. Incubators are not toys. Don't turn over a man's work to a boy.

34. Don't expect to hatch without work. The man who expects to get chicks by trusting to the regulator to keep the heat regular does not deserve success. Work is required for other stock that need winter care, and the artificial hen is no exception.

Hen's or Duck's Eggs.—Are the conditions the same with the incubators in hatching duck eggs as with hen's eggs? That is, shall I keep the same moisture and heat in the incubator for the duck eggs as for the hen's eggs?

The conditions are the same, only the duck eggs want but little moisture the first three weeks, really requiring less moisture than hen's eggs. The temperature required is the same.

The Best Broilers.—Which are good breeds for broilers?

Plymouth Rock, Brahmas, Cochins, Wyandottes, Langshans and Leghorns, White Wonders and Cornish Indians.

Right Temperature.—Please inform me how hot or cold it must be in the incubator to spoil the eggs.

Lower than 40 is injurious, and 116 for an hour will spoil them. These are extremes.

No Test for Fertility.—Do you know of any egg tester by which you can tell a fertilized egg before putting in the incubator?

There is no way of knowing if an is egg fertile before being used for incubation.

Cellar for an Incubator.—Will a damp cellar do for an incubator?

Yes. In a damp cellar you will not need any moisture pans in the machine, as the natural moisture of the cellar air will be sufficient. But a dry cellar is the best.

Chicks in Brooder.—How long should chickens be kept in the brooder before they can do without artificial heat?

Until about eight or ten weeks old, but it depends on the season and weather. The rule is to keep them in the brooder until they are well feathered.

Size of Brooder House.—What should be the size of a house in which to raise 75 to 100 chicks to three pounds, and will a house built of rough boards, and covered with good roofing, be warm enough?

A house 10x12, divided into two pens 6x10, will do very well. A brooder will comfortably accommodate 50 to 60 chicks till eight or ten weeks old, at which age they should be ready for market.

Chicks Dead in Shell.—I am using an incubator and have had very good success until recently. Now I find many full grown chicks dead in the shell. What is the cause?

Too much heat probably, although it is not certain that it is the fault of the incubator; the same thing happens sometimes with hens. No one has yet found out why chicks die in the shell.

Heat at 106 Degrees.—Will it do harm to have the heat rise to 106 degrees in an incubator after the eggs have been in three days or more?

It will cause the chicks to hatch a day or two earlier than they should if the heat is too high, but a temperature of 106 degrees for a short time will do but little injury.

A 400-Egg Machine.—Give dimensions for a 400-egg hot-water incubator. Is it necessary to have the tank proportionately larger than a 100-egg incubator?

To estimate the capacity, allow four square inches for each egg. Hence tank for 400-egg incubator should be 1600 square inches or 40x40 inches. If preferred it may be about 35x45 or of any shape desired.

Measurement of Moisture.—Can I get too much moisture in the machine? After the eggs had been in three days I set two baking pans of water under the egg trays and sprinkled the eggs twice a day.

Never sprinkle eggs as the constant chilling twice a day to which you subjected the eggs probably killed the germs; some early, others half grown, and others which were hardier and stronger, survived nearly long enough to escape. A few sponges are sufficient for moisture.

How Much Moisture.—How often, how much and what time should moisture be put in a two-lamp incubator? Capacity, 200 eggs.

The measurement of moisture is impossible. Water evaporates more rapidly when warm than when cold. Everything depends on how much air flows in, the temperature, stage of incubation, cubic inches of space in incubator, etc. No one can know how much moisture to give. It can only be determined by observation during the hatch. Some incubators are now run without moisture.

Brooder House.—How many chicks would a brooder house 50 feet long and 12 feet wide accommodate? Could I heat it with a stove?

It may hold 500 if divided into 10 apartments of 5 feet by 8, leaving a 3 foot walk on the north side. That would give you ten brooders which would accommodate 50 chicks each. You would have a stove with a water jacket and outflow and return pipes for the hot water, as an ordinary stove will not answer. You should have the heat where it keeps the chicks warm and hot water pipes are excellent.

Temperature for Hatching.—Will eggs hatch with a constant temperature of 100 to 102 degrees?

It is rather low, as the hatch will be delayed and the chicks weakened somewhat. The nearer the temperature is kept to 103 degrees the better.

Ruffled Feathers—What is the cause of incubator chicks being ruffled in feathers? Some act as if benumbed, stretch out their necks, and lay down?

May be due to several causes—bottom heat, lice, dampness or insufficient heat in brooder, as a rule the lack of warmth being the cause.

Moisture.—If I keep a pan of water in my incubator and wet sponges under the egg-drawer, (which has a cloth bottom) is there any need of keeping wet sponges in with the eggs?

Sponges are sufficient without the water pans. Eggs really need little or no moisture during incubation.

When to Begin.—How early can I start an incubator, and will I have to keep it where it won't freeze, or would it be better to let the hens set and take care of the chicks that early?

October is usually the time to begin. It should be in a place of moderate temperature. You cannot use hens that early, as they may not be broody.

Too High Temperature.—If eggs get too hot in an incubator, should they be sprinkled with warm water to cool them? Are eggs roasted if the heat reaches 110 degrees?

A temperature of 110 degrees is not necessarily fatal unless continued for too long a time. Cool the eggs by simply leaving the egg drawer open.

Handling—Does it do harm to handle the eggs, such as testing them, or changing them from one machine to another after they have been in the incubator three days?

No. Not if they are handled carefully and not exposed to cold air too long. In testing eggs in a cool room it is well to warm a couple of blankets folded to be a little larger than the egg tray. Cover the untested eggs with one warm blanket and spread the other over another tray and slip the eggs under as fast as tested. In this way chilling the eggs can be avoided.

RULES ON RAISING BROILERS.

1. If the chicks do not come out of the eggs until the 22d day, or longer, it indicates that the temperature of the egg drawer was too low. They should begin to pip on the twentieth day.

2. If they begin to come out on the eighteenth day, it indicates that the average temperature was too high.

3. If the chicks come out weak, it indicates either too high or too low temperature, or that the eggs were from immature pullets or over fat hens.

4. Give no feed for thirty-six hours after the chicks are hatched.

5. They should then be fed every two hours until one week old. After that time feed them four times a day until a month old, when three times a day will suffice.

6. Keep a little box of ground charcoal, one of clean ground bone, and one of small sharp flint before them, with plenty of coarse sharp sand on the floor. Also a box of ground oyster shells, as grit, but in recommending these substances, it may be stated, that any kind of sharp small grit will answer.

7. The first feeding may be of rolled oats (dried slightly on the stove if the weather is damp) rubbed between the hands to crumble it. The rolled (or flake) oats are ready prepared, cooked, and can be had of any grocer, being the prepared oatmeal for instantaneous preparation of oatmeal gruel. Feed them to the chicks dry. Stale bread moistened with milk may also be given.

8. On the third day after beginning to feed, vary the food by giving the rolled oats one meal, and prepared cake the next. The prepared cake is made by using equal parts of bran ground corn and oats (corn and oats are usually ground together) and middlings (shipstuff), which should be salted to season it, intimately mixed, and cooked in a pan in the stove oven. Sift the corn and oats first, and feed the coarse parts to fowls. If fresh milk can be had, the food may be mixed with it before cooking. If not, use water. Crumble the cake fine when feeding. It should be fed dry.

9. Ground meat is sometimes used for chicks, but results show that too much of it causes bowel disease. If a piece of lean butcher's meat be cooked to pieces (or chopped fine after cooking), and fed twice a week, it will be sufficient. A gill of linseed meal to every quart of the dry mixture (for making the prepared cake) given once a week, will be beneficial.

10. After the first week any kind of feed, such as mashed potatoes, cooked turnips, crumbled bread of any kind, or any wholesome feed, will be of advantage.

11. When ten days old, the rolled oats may be omitted, and wheat one day and cracked corn the next may be used. Begin to teach chicks to eat wheat and cracked corn early by sprinkling a little on the floor (about a tablespoonful daily) after they are a week old.

12. Young chicks do not eat much at a time, but they eat often. Do not omit a meal. Feed at regular hours.

13. After the chicks are three weeks old, the cake may be omitted, the feed being scalded instead, but the quantity of bran should be reduced one-half.

14. Bran is indigestible if fed raw, and sometimes causes bowel disease, but if cooked, or well scalded, so as to soften it, the bran makes good feed as it largely abounds in the phosphates being the best bone forming element that can be given.

15. A chick must not be even dampened. Water should be given in a manner that only the beak of the chick can become wet. The chicks must not be allowed to tread in the water. Dampness is fatal.

16. A young chick is naked, like a babe just born, the down being no protection, hence everything depends on plenty of heat. Better have the brooder too hot than too cold. If the chicks are with hens, they must have a warm, light place as a hen cannot raise chicks in winter any better than it can be done artificially, as it is not her natural period of the year for so doing.

17. No thermometer is needed in the brooder, or under the hen. If the chicks crowd together especially at night, they need more warmth. When they shove their heads out of

the sides of the brooder, or from under the hen, the heat is just right. Whenever the chicks do not sleep near the edges of the brooder, but get as close to each other as possible, give more heat.

18. When the chicks show signs of leg weakness, have clogging of the vent, and bowel disease results, there is a lack of warmth in the brooder, especially at night. The night is when the chicks meet with the greater number of difficulties.

19. When chickens have leg weakness and the floor of the brooder is very warm, the cause is too much bottom heat. Bottom heat is excellent for chicks until they are a week old, but after that time there should be only warmth enough on the floor to not have the floor cold. All warmth should come over the chicks. They feel the warmth on the backs with more satisfaction than on any other portion of the body.

20. When the chicks have good appetites but have leg weakness, the chicks moving on their knees but otherwise appear lively, it denotes rapid growth, and is not necessarily fatal. Follow directions in No. 17 above.

21. Feed the chicks on clean surfaces or in little troughs, never leave food to ferment. Clean off the brooders and floors daily. Keep dry earth in the corner of the brooder house for the chicks to dust in.

22. When you see the chicks busy and scratching, it is a sign of thrift.

23. A single night may ruin all. Never let the brooder become cold for an hour. Once the chicks get chilled they never fully recover.

24. When the chicks seem to be continually crying it means more warmth needed. The warmth is more important than the food.

25. If the chicks are stupid, drowsy, continually cry, or have fits look on the heads and necks, and under the wings for the large lice. Also examine for little red mites.

26. Never feed raw cornmeal to very young chicks. Crumbled stale bread is always good for them.

27. Clover hay, cut very fine, and steeped in boiling water over night, and sprinkled with cornmeal slightly, fed three times a week, is excellent, but unless it is exceedingly fine the chicks cannot eat it. One of the best invigorators, however, is the decoction from the clover (clover tea), given in the place of drinking water occasionally, but it must be fresh.

28. Drinking water in winter should be tepid, not cold, and fresh and clean.

29. Feed very early in the morning as soon as the chicks come out of the brooder. Never keep them waiting for breakfast.

30. Milk may be given, but should be fresh, and the residuum carefully removed, but do not substitute it for water. Give water to the chicks from the start. Curds may be given two or three times a week. Also fresh buttermilk. Milk, however, is not necessary where it is difficult to procure.

31. A chick should weigh a pound when five weeks old. The average is a pound at six weeks old. It should be ready for market when eight weeks old. To fatten for market give plenty of wheat and cracked corn.

32. The White or Brown Leghorn male crossed with Brahma, Cochin, Wyandotte, Langshan, Dorking or Plymouth Rock hens, or grades, make excellent broilers. For choice quality broilers use Pit Game male on Dorking hens. The Houdan crosses on large hens, produce fine broilers. The Wyandotte and Plymouth Rock males are excellent. The best results in hatching are when the Leghorn male is used.

33. Hatching should begin in October and end in April or May. The best prices are obtained in April and May.

34. It costs five cents in food to raise one pound of chick. The cost of eggs, labor, building, etc , are extra. The heaviest cost is in the eggs (which are high in winter) as they often fail to hatch.

35. Hens are better than pullets for producing broilers. The males should not be less than ten months old.

36. Eggs from molting hens, immature pullets, or from hens in the yards with cocks having frosted combs, chilled eggs, very small eggs, will not give good results.

37. In a majority of cases the failure is due to the eggs and not to the incubator.

38. Read these rules once a day until you can repeat them from memory. Then keep your eyes on the chicks.

POINTS IN FAVOR OF THE INCUBATOR AND BROODER.

1. Ten to fifty times more eggs can be hatched by one machine, in the same length of time, than by one hen; and at the same time, require no more attention than the hen.

2. It is an easier and more agreeable job to turn the eggs and fill the lamp daily, of an incubator, than it is to lift a cross and fussy hen from the nest, feed her and watch that she returns to duty at the proper time.

3. An incubator will not trample on and break the eggs, as is nearly always the case, more or less with a sitting hen.

4 It is a difficult matter to keep lice and mites from attacking and multiplying on the sitting hen, which is, to say the least, a source of great annoyance to the hen. There is no chance for such a state of affairs in an incubator. These little pests won't germinate and grow fat on ash or oak boards.

5. The inclination of an incubator to become broody does not have to be consulted, as is the case with the hen. Give it the eggs, light the lamp, and the machine is your obedient servant for as long a period as its services are required.

6 The machine will not become weak or emaciated from over-work; and chicks can thus be hatched out for months at a stretch.

7. There is more pleasure and fewer vexatious trials in operating an incubator than there is in steering to victory an obstinate and vicious hen

8. Home made brooders are quite common, and a person with a fair supply of ingenuity can construct one that will answer very well in many respects. It is a dumb but perfect mother, and it is amusing to see how the young chicks take to it. Some of the advantages of brooders are:

1. Snug and secure quarters are ever ready for the young chicks when taken from the incubator.

2. Two hundred chicks can be handled and cared for in one-tenth the time it would require were they with the hens.

3. The chicks can be fed more regularly and much more evenly, and are less liable to disease and accident; and raids from "varmints" and reptiles are impossible.

4. The chicks can be kept dry and comfortable at all times, and this, too, with one-fourth the attention necessary where they are running with hens.

5. It is almost impossible for lice and mites to attack the chicks, for there is no cause for parasites of this nature to get a start.

6. Chicks reared in this way become very docile, and are consequently much easier handled when they mature.

7. There is five times more pleasure attached to rearing chicks in a brooder than otherwise.

8. Everyone who raises chicks should have a brooder whether they have an incubator or not. The chicks can be taken from the hens and put in the brooder and the hens reset. A brooder is a household necessity. And they are cheap.

CHAPTER VI.

Miscellaneous Inquiries.

Limber Neck.—What is Limber Neck? How can it be cured?

This is an affliction native to the South. The birds which have it act as though they were drunk. They reel, twist their heads about, fall backwards, stagger, fall down and get up, eat and are apparently all right for a little while, when another spasm will seize them. Limber neck is the St. Vitus' dance of chickendom. Having been raised where this ailment occasionally appears, the writer of this never heard of but one remedy said to be efficient, and that is a pill of asafetida the size of a pea, giving night and morning, feeding same as usual Sometimes a fowl with limber neck will live a month or more, but it kills them finally if not relieved. No one knows the origin or cause of limber neck.

Ridge on Egg Shells.—Will you please tell me what causes a ridge around an egg shell?

No one knows. It just happens and the next egg the hen lays will be all right

Good Hatch.—What is considered a good hatch from 13 eggs?

One more than half—hence seven chicks are considered a good hatch from 13 eggs.

White on Black Minorcas.—Do Black Minorcas have any white on them?

When very young, some of the down is white. Adult fowls occasionally have a little white on their plumage, but lose it at molting time.

Mating Dark and Light.—Which is best to mate, dark roosters and light hens, or light roosters and dark hens, both for looks and profit? They are Plymouth Rock fowls.

The light males and medium dark hens are usually preferred.

Hatching Bantams.—When should Bantams be hatched?

August should be the last month. Hatch Bantams from March till August. A secret in the breeding of this variety of birds is to keep them down in size. If got out early in the season, they grow finely all summer, and may get some ounces heavier at maturity, of either sex, than if bred later in the season.

Shipping Coops.—How many inches wide, long and high should a shipping coop be for one or two fowls?

That depends upon the size of the fowls. We advise to give about a square foot of floor space to each, when shipping a number. For instance, a coop 2 feet wide by 3 feet long, contains six square feet, and will do very well for six fowls as Plymouth Rocks or Wyandottes; would carry eight or ten Leghorns or Hamburgs; or four or five Cochins or Brahmas. For height:—they should be high enough to allow the birds to stand erect without touching the top. Many breeders make a mistake in this and ship birds, especially cockerels, in too low coops.

Capons.—How should capons be fed in the winter months? Do they need outside yards? How many can be kept in a building 15x80 feet? How much room will I need to winter 200?

Simply keep them growing. Feed on any food they will eat, but do not get them too fat until near time for selling. A very small yard will answer—just enough to allow of some outdoor air and exercise. About 100 can be kept in that size building, but they may be crowded more if building is kept clean and the weather is cold. It is usual to allow four square feet for each bird, or 800 square feet for 200 birds.

Cross Breeding.—What breed should be crossed on White Leghorn hens to produce a good laying fowl? Would Plymouth Rocks do? What color would the cross be, and would they be non-sitters?

You would find some difficulty in *crossing up* a small variety like the White Leghorns from the female side. The color would probably be mixed, and they would be sitters, the crossing of two non-sitting varieties will produce sitters, the act of crossing seeming to develop that instinct, presumably latent until stimulated into activity by the cross-breeding. Otherwise there is no difficulty in affecting a cross. The best cross for eggs is a Brown Leghorn male with Partridge Cochin hen. Crosses do not equal pure breeds.

Egg Tester.—How can I make a good egg tester?

To make an egg tester to use with a common lamp, take a pasteboard box about seven inches long and six inches wide and six inches deep. Cut a hole in the bottom big enough to fit the large part of a lamp chimney through. Next cut a hole about the shape of an egg, but rather smaller, in one end so that it will be opposite to the lamp flame when the tester is slipped over the chimney. Cover the box outside with any dull, black cloth, so that no light can get through, and you are ready for business. Light the lamp, place the tester in position, and the egg over the oval opening in the side. Turn it gently as you look, and its condition will be clearly exposed to view.

Lime, Gravel, Oyster Shells.—Is lime and gravel as good as oyster shells?

Gravel, sea shells, or hard dry bone will answer. Shells serve more as grit than any other purpose.

Bolton Grays—Will you please say if there is such a fowl as Bolton Grays?

The old Bolton Grays have now become the Silver Penciled and Silver Spangled Hamburgs.

White Minorcas.—Will you please give the origin of the White Minorcas?

They are of Spanish origin, coming first from the island of Minorca, from which they derived the name.

Value of Alfalfa.—How does alfalfa compare with clover as an egg producing food?

It is fully equal to clover in every respect.

Fattening Cockerels—How do you fatten cockerels from late hatch, Plymouth Rocks?

Feed on plenty of corn with soft feed three times a day.

A Good Cross.—What do you think of crossing Plymouth Rocks with Games, and are they as good as the pure bred Plymouth Rocks?

The cross of Indian game and Plymouth Rock will produce a grand table fowl, and cannot be surpassed.

Highest Egg Record.—Please give me the highest egg record for a hen in one year?

In England 280 is claimed, but we have no records, and cannot state. Be satisfied with 150 or even 100.

Pulling the Primaries.—If I pull the primary feathers out of fowls' wings, will they grow in again all right?

If pulled they begin to grow at once. If cut they do not renew until the bird molts.

Chicks from Small Eggs.—Will birds hatched from the small eggs be as large as those from large ones produced by another hen?

Yes, as small eggs do not mean that a hen will not lay them larger, but it is safer to breed from hens that lay large eggs uniformly.

Bone.—I am a beginner and want to ask if burnt bone is as good as raw bone.

Burning the bone causes a loss of the nitrogen, (cartilage, meat, etc.) but the lime and phosphates remain. The raw bone is better.

The Standard.—What is the book called "The Standard?"

It is a volume prepared by a society of poultrymen known as "The American Poultry Association." Its title is *"The American Standard of Perfection."* It is not a treatise on poultry culture, but merely describes, point by point, each recognized variety of fowls. It's cost is $1.00.

About the Polish.—Does a pure White Crested Black Polish get white feathers through the body when it is two or three years old?

The color should be black with no white through the body; but it often happens that aged birds show white feathers, as the tendency is to grow lighter with age.

Leghorn Combs.—How many points must any variety of Leghorn hens have on their combs, provided there are no side sprigs, or is it immaterial?

Five or six—five preferred, for all varieties of Leghorns. We presume the same for the Browns, but the standard does not specify number.

Eating Pumpkin Seeds.—How do you account for fowls eating pumpkin seeds, getting giddy or drunk, and ultimately dying in that condition?

That they are injurious has been demonstrated, but the cause is unknown, due probably to some active principle in the seeds.

Best Chick Feed.—Let me know what to feed to young chicks of the breeds that feather fast, to prevent drooping of wings and in many instances dying?

Begin with pin head oat meal for very young chicks. When they begin to feather keep them warm, feed four times a day, and give oat meal, wheat and corn meal, often.

Buy or Raise.—Isn't it cheaper and better for one lacking somewhat in room, to buy pullets at ten cents a pound for laying stock than to raise them?

Raise them always. By raising them you can select the *breed* preferred, which is very important.

Excellent Cross—Please tell me what you think of a cross between White Leghorn and Light Brahma? What would be the advantage of such a cross, and should I use a Leghorn cockerel on Brahma hens, or vice versa?

The cross produces a bird larger than the Leghorn, and more active than the Brahma, the Leghorn predominating. Use the Leghorn male. The cross is an excellent one. But why use a cross?

Egg Shells for Fowls.—Are egg shells good for fowls in winter?

Yes, egg shells are excellent for fowls at any time, but should be smashed fine so as to be readily eaten. Otherwise they may cause the fowls to eat their eggs.

Number of Males, Feed, Etc.—Will one male do with 25 pullets? Is good wheat at $1.00, cheap feed? How much wheat will 25 hens need at a meal?

Two males should be used if on a range. One quart of wheat, with bone and clover is sufficient. See articles on "Feeding," elsewhere in this book.

Laying after Molting—What time do hens generally begin laying after molting?

That depends upon how they have been fed previously. If fed for eggs, they will take but a short recess for molting, sometimes none at all. If the system is exhausted, the molt (producing a new suit of clothes) is a heavy drain upon a hen, and she may not get built up to laying vigor again before spring.

Three Classes—According to utility, how should the various breeds be classified?

The utility of the breeds can be divided into three classes, as follows: For egg farming—Leghorns, Minorcas, Hamburgs, Andalusians, Anconas, Spanish and Houdans. Second. For table birds (roasters)—Dorkings and Games. For market, Brahmas, Cochins, Plymouth Rocks, Wyandottes, Langshans and White Wonders.

A Durable Whitewash.—Will you give a recipe for a durable whitewash?

One half bushel of good lime, five pounds rock salt, dissolve; one-half pound of whiting, four pounds ground rice boiled to a thin paste; one-half pound clean grease. Slake the lime in a tight box or barrel with hot water, keeping the box covered that the steam may not escape. Slake to the consistency of thick cream. Thin it when used, so that it will flow freely from the brush. If put on too thick it will flake off more or less when dry. The above is for outside work. For indoors slake the lime as above with hot water, omitting the salt, grease and rice. Instead of thinning the creamy solution with water, use skim milk.

Pullets for Broilers.—Would you recommend me to get last year's hens, or pullets of this year, to hatch broilers, and for winter eggs?

Pullets (or a male) hatched not later than April, would probably answer, but we think stock over one year old better.

Broody Hens.—What is the best method of breaking up broody hens?

Shut them in a pen by themselves, away from nests, two or three days. If you have a spare cock, or lively young cockerel, put him in with them.

Excrement on Chicks—What is the cause of the excrement of incubator-hatched chicks hanging on posteriors and hardening there?

It is the result of bowel disease, and may be noticed on chicks with hens also. Remove it and anoint parts with a few drops of sweet oil.

Profit in Bantams.—Do you consider the raising of Bantams at all profitable? Are their eggs salable?

Being small, the eggs are not always salable, but in proportion to cost of keep, (and size of eggs in proportion to size of fowl), they are more profitable for home use than any other breed.

How Old.—Is there any way to tell the difference in the age of a one-year old hen and a two-year-old hen?

The hen has a more fully developed body, the legs are rougher, and some of them have spurs quite long. The older the hen the more likely the comb and wattles are rough or injured, while the general plumage is not as clear and bright as that of a young hen, nor the older hens as active or sprightly.

Describe Partridge Cochins.—Will you please give me a description of Partridge Cochins? What should be the color of the plumage, earlobes, legs, and should the leg and middle toe be covered with feathers in order to be full blood?

Head red, comb single, earlobes red, neck red with black stripe down middle of feather, back same, breast black, tail black, legs yellow and feathered on outside to end of outer toe—middle toe feathered.

Toasted Corn.—I am feeding corn toasted, every other night; will that made hens lay?

Yes, provided you give a variety of feed also.

Fit for Service.—At what age is a healthy Leghorn cockerel fit for breeding purposes?

A Leghorn cockerel matures early. He is serviceable when six months old.

How to Ship Broilers.—Please give the best way to prepare and ship broilers to New York in winter and summer—1000 miles.

Simply dry pick them, removing only the feathers, pack in barrels, and send by express. In summer it is best not to ship so far.

Late in Maturing.—I have two Wyandot cockerels. They are over five months old and have never crowed. They are healthy, vigorous birds. What is the matter with them? Will they do to breed from?

They are only slow in maturing, and will probably be of large size. They will crow soon enough, and can be used for breeding purposes.

The Dunghills.—What is the average number of eggs laid by a dunghill fowl in a year, with reasonable good care and feed?

No two dunghills are alike, hence there are a thousand, (or more) kinds of dunghills. They will sometimes do well with good care, but seldom exceed 80 or 100 eggs per year.

Plaster and Manure.—Which is the best way to save poultry manure? Will it pay to buy land plaster to put under the roosts? I have board platforms under the roosts and scatter lime and dust, clean every few days and pack in barrels. Will it do to keep the barrel out of doors well covered with boards?

Plaster is excellent and cheap. Omit the lime, as it causes loss of ammonia. Otherwise your method is correct. Manure should be kept dry, but the boards will answer if they do not admit moisture. Some prefer to keep it moist with soapsuds.

Combs of Brown Leghorns.—Please describe the combs of Single-Combed Brown Leghorns, male and female, for breeders?

Comb is single; has five points. Comb of male should be erect, and that of the female should droop to one side.

Carbolic Acid.—Is carbolic acid good in the water for chickens?

Carbolic acid is good for some purposes, but should not be used in the water.

About Broilers.—In crossing sitting and non sitting breeds, which would you use for the top cross? Also, what variety would you breed for very early broilers?

Always use a male from the non-sitting breed. Small males with large hens is the rule.

Crossing for Eggs.—I have Single Comb Brown Leghorn hens, and would like to cross them to improve their egg production and size. How do you think it would do to use a silver Spangled Hamburg or Black Minorca cock?

Nothing is gained by crossing, as it destroys the good qualities of both parents. You cannot improve the egg production of Leghorns by crossing.

White Black Spanish.—I have a W. F Black Spanish hen that about the first of December began changing color, molting her black feathers and growing white ones, until now she is half white. Can you explain it?

No, it is simply a freak of nature.

Dubbing.—Will you explain the operation of "dubbing?"

The operation of dubbing is easily performed. The right age is when the chicks are from ten to twelve weeks old, or when the comb has made a good start to grow out. A sharp pair of shears is the best instrument to use; trim the comb close to the head with one clip of the shears, and one clip for each wattle, and it is done The operation should be performed in the evening, after the fowls have gone to roost, as then the few drops of blood drawn will dry up, and the cuts be seared over before morning. Use no hot iron, grease, or wash of any kind, and the fowls will go about their business the next day, as though nothing had happened. We do not approve of the practice, as it is cruel.

Every Day Layers.—What breed of hens will lay every day? Some think that Brahmas crossed with Plymouth Rocks will lay every day, and chickens come early also.

There is no breed of fowls that will lay every day. If one gets them to lay 200 eggs a piece in a year he does exceedingly well.

To Dilute Carbolic Acid.—What will cut crude carbolic acid so it can be diluted or make it into a powder similar to what is sold at the stores? What is understood by crude petroleum and where can it be gotten?

Dissolve in warm water and use the water for slaking lime. Crude petroleum is the unrefined article, and should be obtained at any drug store.

Chicks Die in the Shell.—Why do chicks die in the shell after pipping, and just before time to come out?

No one knows why chicks die in the shell. There are many theories, but no one knows.

How to Kill Fowls.—Is there any better way of killing fowls for the table than by cutting off their heads?

Cutting off the head insures thorough bleeding for one thing, which cutting across the roof of the mouth does not *surely* do, and this thorough bleeding is a very important part of the wholesomeness of the meat. If the severed neck is unsightly, the skin can be drawn over the end and tied with a bit of cord, concealing the ragged neck.

Chemistry of Egg Shells.—Of what is the shell of eggs composed?

A writer in *Popular Science Monthly* says: "The shell proper of an egg is made up mostly of earthy materials. The proportions vary according to the food of the bird, but 90 to 97 per cent is carbonate of lime. The remainder is composed of from two to five per cent. of animal matter and from one to five per cent. of phosphate of lime and magnesia. Now, some one asks. where does the hen procure the carbonate of lime with which to form the shell? If we confine fowls in a room and feed them with any of the cereal grains, excluding all sand. dust. or earthy matter, they will go on for a time and lay eggs, each one having a perfect shell, made up of the same calcareous elements. Vauquelin shut up a hen for ten days and fed her exclusively upon oats, of which she consumed 7474 grains in weight. During this time four eggs were laid, which weighed nearly 409 grains; of this amount 276 grains were carbonate of lime, 17½ grains phosphate of lime and 10 grains gluten. But there is only a little carbonate of lime in oats.

Light Yolks.—Why is it that the yolks of the eggs from my hens are light in color instead of yellow?

It is due to lack of coloring matter in the food, and happens during the cold season. In summer when grass is plentiful, the color will be deeper. The light color is no indication that the eggs are lacking in quality.

Value of Kerosene.—Give us your estimate on the value of kerosene in the poultry yard.

The many uses that kerosene may be put to in the poultry yard make it an indispensible article. For painting the inside of nest boxes for sitting hens there is nothing equal to it, as it surely kills all vermin with which it comes in contact, and prevents other vermin entering the nest until it is entirely evaporated, which, if the crude oil is used, will give the hen amply time to hatch her brood. A few drops in the drinking water occasionally has a good effect upon the general health of the flock, and for colds or roup there is nothing better, if carefully applied.

Crude Carbolic Acid.—I wish to inquire about carbolic acid. I suppose it can be bought in powder, in crystals and in solution. Which is the best way to buy it? How should the powder or crystals be dissolved? What proportion of water? I want to use it about the hennery. "One tablespoonful of carbolic acid to a quart of slacked lime." Does this mean the acid in powder or solution? About how much should I pay for it by the pound?

It is sold in all conditions, crystalized and crude. Also a solution. The crude acid is the kind used. The liquid is of varying strength. An ounce of the crude dissolved in a pint of water answers for ordinary purposes. A tablespoonful of a solution of carbolic acid to a quart of lime will make the carbonate of lime. The crystalized is $1.00 per pound, the liquid (saturated solution) is 60 cents per pound. Crude from 20 to 40 cents.

Frozen Combs.—Are hens with frozen combs as good as those not so injured?

If the combs heal they are not injured as layers. It is only during the time the comb is sore that they will not lay. A frozen comb is always unsightly.

Space per Fowl.—How many square feet to each fowl should be allowed?

The rule is to allow a house 5 x10 feet for ten hens, which gives each hen 5 square feet. In the winter a number of fowls may be together. The space applies to the square feet on the floor of the house only. The yard should be ten times as large as house if possible.

New Blood.—*July Hatch.*—1. Would it injure the progeny, in fine markings and egg production, to cross a cock of a particular strain of another strain, all being of the same breed? 2. Would Leghorn chicks, hatched in July, be matured in December, About what month would their eggs be fertile?

1. It would be an advantage to do so if careful selection was made. Of course, to preserve markings the parents must be well marked. 2. Leghorn pullets often begin to lay when five months old, hence your pullets may begin in December, but the eggs may not all be fertile.

Preserving Green Food for the Winter.—How can a silo be made for ensilage for fowls?

A silo is simply a strong, air-tight box, pit or hogshead—in fact, anything that will answer the purpose—and ensilage is green food such as grass, vegetable tops, growing corn or any substance that will be relished by poultry. For poultry, a strong barrel or hogshead will answer. The green food should not be cut until it is near maturity, or it will be largely composed of water. If cut just before ripening, the elements intended for the formation of seeds will be arrested in the stalks, and ensilage will be more nutritious. Pass the material through a cutter to get it into half inch lengths. Pack it close and tight in the barrel, and place the head of the barrel on the ensilage. The head should be just small enough to go down *into* the barrel. On the barrel-head place stones, or any kind of weight, so that when the contents of the barrel are compressed and sink, the head of the barrel will sink with it. As the contents go down, add more ensilage until the barrel is full. The heavy pressure will exclude the air, and the contents can be kept in an excellent state of preservation.

Temperature for House.—Should a chicken house be warm enough so it will not freeze for hens to lay well, and should they be allowed to run, or shut up in pens ?

About 40 degrees above zero is not too cold. The hens may be allowed to run out at will, as they will be governed by instinct, but should be kept shut up on raw, damp days.

Net Profit per Hen.—What is the net profit to be reasonably expected per hen?

Experiments made in different sec tions show that the cost of feeding a hen one year is about $1, and that the profit is about the same, the gross receipts from the hen being about $2 a year. Of course, this varies according to the breed, cost of food and location being more and sometimes less ; but it is accepted that $1 pays the cost and $1 profit is made from each hen.

Preserving the Droppings.—What is the most practical way of keeping the droppings until they can be applied to the soil ?

The best way to preserve them is to clean out the house every alternate day. Mix one bushel dry earth, one bushel droppings, and half a peck of kainit (crude German potash salts) together, and put away in a dry place. Kainit can be bought by the bag at any fertilizer store, and is not only cheap, but of itself a good potash fertilizer. In the mixture it forms sulphates, and fixes the ammonia. If it cannot be procured, use dry land plaster instead, but kainit is much better. Keep the mixture moist.

Changing Males.—Is it necessary to change male birds, and how often ?

Keep them several seasons if vigorous. Do not change oftener than necessary and do not be afraid of inbreeding.

The Dorking—Why do the Americans give the Dorkings such little attention? In England it is more highly prized than any other fowl.

The Dorking is one of the best of fowls and thrives best in England, for reasons not well understood, as they make hardy fowls in this country when matured, but the chicks are hard to raise. A cross of the Dorking and Brahma, however, makes a fowl compact in form, plump and well adapted to America.

Mixing the Breed.—I have some Langshans that have run with a mixed flock. I want to mate them with a Langshan cock; how long before I can have pure eggs?

About ten days is allowed, but a month is safer.

Litter in Brooder Runs.—What should be used for litter in brooders and runs, and is sawdust objectionable?

Do not use sawdust, as chicks will sometimes fill their crops with sawdust. For very small chicks, bran is more suitable.

Green Bones, Etc.—1. How often should green bones be fed, and how much to ten hens? 2. How often, and how much, to growing chicks? 3. Is it better to keep the pullets from other fowls? 4. Which is the better way to feed clover to laying hens— to cure it and steam it, or feed it green? 5. Will young ducks thrive in brooders as well as with hens?

1. Feed one pound a day to sixteen hens. 2. Keep it before the chicks all the time. 3. It is better to keep them separate. 4. Feed it green in summer and cured in winter. 5. They thrive fully as well in brooders.

Standard Weights.—Please give the Standard weights for the various breeds of fowls.

The following table gives the information in concise form:—

BREED.	COCK.	COCK'L.	HEN.	PUL.
Lt. Brahma	12 lbs.	10 lbs.	9½ lbs.	8 lbs.
Dark do	11 "	9 "	8½ "	7 "
All Cochins	11 "	9 "	8½ "	7 "
Langshan	9½ "	8 "	7 "	6 "
All P. Rocks	9½ "	8 "	7½ "	6¼ "
All Wyandots	8½ "	7½ "	6½ "	5½ "
All Javas	10 "	8½ "	8 "	6½ "
W. Dorkings	7½ "	6½ "	6 "	5 "
S. G. do	8 "	7 "	6½ "	5½ "
Colored do	9½ "	8 "	7½ "	6 "
All Minorcas	8 "	6½ "	6½ "	5½ "
Red Caps	7½ "	6 "	6½ "	5 "
Am. Dominique	8½ "	7½ "	6½ "	5½ "
Houdans	7 "	6 "	6 "	5 "
La Fleche	8½ "	7½ "	7½ "	6½ "
Creve Cœur	8 "	7 "	7 "	6 "

If they are under the following weights they are disqualified and cannot compete in any well-regulated exhibition, viz :

BREED.	COCK.	COCK'L.	HEN.	PUL.
Lt. Brahma	9 lbs.	7½ lbs.	7½ lbs.	6 lbs.
Dark do	9 "	7½ "	7 "	5 "
All Cochins	7 "	7 "	8 "	5½ "
Langshans	8½ "	6½ "	7 "	5 "

Maturity of Hamburgs.- I have Silver Spangled Hamburg chicks hatched the latter part of April. Will they be matured by the 15th of September?

They should be matured by September, as the small breeds mature quickly.

About Crosses.—If I should cross single-comb birds with rose comb, what would be the result? 2. Are there rose-comb Minorcas? 3. Are eggs from cross breeds ever sold for hatching? How much are they worth? 4. What is the standard weight of Langshans and of Minorcas? 5. Do Minorcas lay as large eggs as the Leghorns?

1. The result will be both rose and single-comb chicks. 2. Yes. 3. Very seldom. Not much. 4. Langshan male nine and one-half pounds; Minorca male eight pounds. 5. Yes.

Brown Eggs and Non Sitters —Do all non-sitters lay white eggs?

It is, perhaps, something curious that all the non-sitting breeds lay eggs that are pure white in color. The brown eggs come from the large Asiatic breeds, though the eggs from Wyandottes, Langshans and Plymouth Rocks are somewhat dark. While some of our enterprising breeders are working on the production of meritorious new breeds, they might find it profitable to turn their attention to the establishment of a non-sitting breed which will lay brown eggs. It is a wide field in which to work, and, as nothing seems impossible with this generation, success may be attained. It is safe to state that when a non-sitting breed (Leghorns, for instance), is introduced that lays brown eggs, the originator will find himself well taxed to fill the orders that will be poured in upon him.

Eggs or Broilers.—Which does it pay best to produce, eggs or broilers?

The fact is that *both* pay best. If you expect to make eggs pay and not keep the *egg-producing breeds*, you will not be so successful. But *which* are the egg-producing breeds? They are those breeds that are kept in full exercise, and not over fed, and which are *hardy* according to the climate. Do not lose sight of that one quality *hardiness*. The best breed in New England is not the best breed in Florida. The best breed for confinement is not the best

on the range. Where the winters are cold and long such breeds as the Brahamas, Cochins, Plymouth Rocks, Langshans, Wyandottes, and even Leghorns, will serve well, and in more moderate climates the Leghorns, Hamburgs, Games, Black Spanish and Minorcas will give good results, but in cold climates, with good care, they will also be profitable. The man who finds no money in eggs is the one who does not improve his stock.

SEVERAL QUERIES.

Would Leghorns crossed with Dorkings make good broilers? (Yes). —At what age should chicks of the large breeds be allowed to roost without danger of crooked breast bone? (When about five months old).—At what age should Light Brahma pullets begin to lay? (About eight months).—Are Minorcas non-sitters? (Yes).—Should pepper be given to fowls? (No). What makes eggs sometimes look "white livered?" (It is on account of the feed. Give some fresh meat and clover) —What is "vulture hock?" (Stiff projecting feathers at the hock joint).—Should all eggs from the same breed of fowls be of the same color? (Not necessarily).—Will coal ashes take the place of road dust for a bath? (Yes).—Is unslacked lime injurious to fowls if they eat it? (No).—Will pullets begin to lay earlier if a cockerel runs with them? (No).—How many fowls are enough to be kept in a building 32x22 ft.? (Fifty, in two pens, 25 in each)— What will take frost out of frozen combs and wattles? (Glycerine put on three times a week)—At what age should a Wyandot cockerel begin to crow? (Sometimes they crow when three months old).—Do pure-bred Wyandots ever throw single combs? (Sometimes, but rarely). If a rose-comb Leghorn cockerel is mated to single-comb pullet what comb would the offspring have? (Some single, some rose). What is the usual price for incubator-hatched chicks a day old? (Ten cents).—Will hens swallow without injury, large pieces of bone? (Yes, as large as a bean or larger). —How shall I keep sun flower seeds in winter? (Simply in a dry place). —How soon can I tell the chicks that are first-class or not? (Not until nearly grown).—Will the black ever come off the beaks of a Plymouth Rock chick? (Yes).—Is a run 100x50 feet large enough for one cock and ten hens? (Yes).—Would it be best to divide it? (Yes.).—I have a yard, 25x70 feet; my house is about 8x8 feet, how many fowls should I keep? (About 25). Should I keep my hens and pullets in the same yard? (Better keep them separate).—Will pullets hatched last April do to breed from this Spring? (They will).

POINTS ON LICE.

1. When chicks droop, and appear sick without cause, especially in summer, look for lice (not for little red mites), but the large grey body lice on the heads and necks.

2. If you find them use a few drops of grease of any kind. A teaspoonful of oil of pennyroyal to a cup of lard is excellent.

3. Look under the wings for the red lice, but use only a few drops of the lard.

4. Never grease the bodies of chicks unless lightly, as grease will often kill them.

5. Never use kerosene on chicks, unless it be a teaspoonful of kerosene to a teacup of lard, as it is irritating.

6. Crude petroleum is always excellent, and serves as a liniment, but mix it with twice its quantity of lard.

7. Keep the dust bath always ready. Use dry dirt and sifted coal ashes. Add carbolate of lime,

Persian insect powder, or oil pennyroyal to the dirt.

8. To rid the house of lice, sprinkle coal oil *everywhere*—floor, walls, roosts, yards, roof, inside and outside, and repeat often.

9. Dust insect powders in the feathers, and be *sure* it is fresh and good.

10. Put insect powder and tobacco dust in the nests. Clean them out every week.

11. Even when no lice may be present use the sprinkler of kerosene at least once a week; and keep the roosts always saturated.

12. No matter how clean things may appear look for the *large* lice on the heads, throats and vents.

13. Lice abound both winter and summer, but more especially in summer.

14. One half the chicks and young turkeys die from lice. Chicks or turkeys with hens or turkeys hens *always* have lice, (either the mites or large lice). Remember *that*.

15. Carbolate of lime is the cheapest powder to use for dusting over the floors and walls.

16. Always aim to get the solutions of powders into the cracks and crevices.

17. The easiest and best way] to whitewash is with a force pump. They are now made to force water from a bucket.

CHAPTER VII.

Turkeys, Ducks and Geese.

TURKEYS.

Number for Setting.—How many eggs should be placed under a Turkey hen?

A good-sized bird will cover 20 eggs.

Sore Eyes in Turkeys—What will cure sore eyes in Turkeys?

It is due to exposure during damp weather. Anoint heads with sweet oil, and keep them warm and sheltered from winds.

Best Variety for the Farm—What breed of turkeys would you advise the farmer to keep?

The Bronze or White Holland, as they are hardier and not so closely inbred as some birds.

Broken Eggs.—What can be done with a turkey hen that has had a broken egg in her over a month? She appears quite and well. Gave her castor oil but it did not relieve her.

Keep her on straw and give her rest. Oil the parts and feed a tablespoonful of linseed meal daily.

Cold in the Head.—My turkeys are all swelled in the head under the eye toward the nose, and they sneeze. Can you tell me what the trouble is, and the cure?

It is probably a cold in the head, caused by exposure to cold storms or draughts, probably from roosting on trees during storms. Anoint heads with sweet oil, and keep the birds sheltered.

Feed for Turks.—What should young turks be fed the first week?

A successful turkey-raiser feeds his chicks during the first eight days on eggs boiled hard and minced; during the second week he adds to this bread-crumbs, chopped with parsley and onions; during the third week he keeps back the eggs, and only continues the bread and the vegetables; afterward, instead of the bread, he gives moistened meal, boiled peas, and above all, millet, of which young turkeys are very fond.

Weight of Bronzes.—What should Bronze turkeys weigh?

Males at six months of age weigh from 18 to 22 pounds. Females 10 to 14 pounds. Mature males 30 to 40 pounds; females 18 to 22 pounds.

Age for Breeding Purposes.—Is a turkey gobbler four or five years old as good for breeding purposes as one a year old?

A gobbler is better at three or four years old as a breeder than a year old bird.

Trouble from Lice.—What ails our young turkeys? They are active and hearty, but in a day or so begin to die. They are hatched by hens and good care is given them?

Look on the heads and necks for the large louse. Grease heads, necks and vents, with a few drops of sweet oil.

Turkeys for Farmers.—Can farmers do much at raising turkeys?

No one can succeed better with turkeys than the farmer if he will bestow upon them a fraction of the care he gives his sheep and cattle. Confinement does not suit them, but give them the run of the farm; while they do no damage to the growing crops they do them much good by their destruction of insects, more especially grasshoppers, that frequently destroy whole fields of grain. When they can get these they require but little other feed, but they should be fed a little grain at night so they will be sure to return home to roost. Fifty or more can be raised on most farms each year without ever missing what it takes to keep them and at Thanksgiving they will bring enough ready cash to buy the winter clothing for an ordinary family, or pay a year's taxes on a farm.

Standard Varieties.—How many varieties does the "Standard" recognize?

Six breeds—the Bronze, White, Black, Buff, Slate and Narragansett.

Best as Breeders.—At what age should breeders be selected?

Do not breed from a yearling gobbler if it can be avoided. Hens should be two years old.

Fattening Turkeys.—State the best feed to fatten turkeys.

To fatten turkeys give them their accustomed range and all the cooked corn, meal and potatoes they will eat up clean twice a day; plenty of grain at night and milk to drink at all times. Mix a little pulverized charcoal in the food once a day. Three weeks of this feeding and your turkeys will be in the best possible condition for the table; that is, if they have been growing and in good condition from the start. Remember that no amount of stuffing for a few weeks just before killing will make a prime, extra-large, table or market bird out of a turkey that has been starved and stunted.

Preparing Turkeys for Market.—Give the best method of preparing turkeys for market·

In marketing turkeys always have them dressed, and be sure that they have been picked when dry. The feathers should be removed while the bird is bleeding, and the drawing done immediately afterwards. The wings should be cut off and the neck bone where the head has been removed so cut that the skin can be readily drawn over it. The neck is then thoroughly washed from blood and wiped dry, after which the skin is tied and trimmed. The remaining work should be done with neatness and thoroughness. Thoughtfulness and good care should be exercised from the first, that the skin is preserved well. This gives the young bird a finished appearance and they will command the best prices. Boxes should be used for packing, and some believe it is profitable to have them made to order. They should hold 150 to 200 pounds each and the birds should be packed without using paper. Sort them carefully, placing the larger and smaller birds in separate boxes. No mixture of qualities should go in one box. Pack the birds closely when thoroughly cold. They should not shake when the cover is nailed down.

CONDENSED HINTS ON TURKEYS.

1. Never let young turkeys get wet. Dampness is fatal.
2. Feed nothing the first twenty-four hours after they are hatched.
3. Before putting them in the coop see that it is *perfectly* clean and free from lice, and dust them *three times* a week with Persian insect powder.
4. Be sure the hen is free from lice. Dust her, too.
5. Look out for *mites* and the large lice on the heads, necks and vents. Grease heads, necks and vents with lard, but avoid kerosene.
6. Nine-tenths of the young turkeys die from *lice*. Remember that.
7. Filth will soon make short work of them. Feed on *clean* surfaces. Give water in a manner so they can only wet their *beaks.*
8. The first week feed a mixture of one egg, beaten, and wheat middlings one part, ground meat one part, corn meal one part, mixed, with salt to taste, and cooked as bread, then crumble for them, with milk or curds so they can drink all they want. Feed every two hours early and late.
9. Give a little raw meat every day; also, *finely* chopped onions, or other tender green food.
10. After the first week keep wheat and ground meat, in boxes, before them all the time, but feed, three times a day, on a mixture of corn meal, wheat middlings, ground oats, cooked, and to which chopped green food is added.

DUCKS.

Eggs Don't Hatch.—I want to know why my duck eggs did not hatch good. I keep from 102 to 104 in an incubator and give them plenty of moisture?

Perhaps you give too much moisture. Duck eggs require but little moisture at first. No more at any time than hen's eggs.

Cholera, Roup and Gapes.—Are ducks liable to cholera, roup, or gapes?

They are exempt from these diseases.

How Many Drakes.—How many drakes should be mated with 24 ducks?

Allow one drake for five or six females.

Ducks as Breeders.—Are ducks as prolific layers as hens; and are they as good breeders?

A duck will lay more eggs than some breeds of hens and her eggs will hatch better.

Young Ducks Eggs.—Will duck eggs hatch as soon as ducks first lay?

It depends on their condition. Sometimes when ducks are very young, their eggs are not perfect.

Weight of Pekins.—What is the average weight of Pekin ducks?

If the ducks in a flock average seven pounds each it will be a good one. Standard weight is 8 pounds for an adult drake and seven pounds for female.

Heat, Water, Etc.—Which is best for young ducks, top heat with cold floor, or bottom heat? If the laying stock have access to river will they do better, the eggs be more fertile, and ducklings stronger, than if they are yarded, with only water to drink?

Top heat is better. The ducks will thrive better on the water, but it will be more difficult to secure the eggs.

Pekin and Aylesbury.—1. What is the difference between the Pekin and Aylesbury duck? 2. How long will eggs be good for hatching after the drake is removed?

The Pekin has an orange colored bill, and legs of a dark orange. The Aylesbury has flesh-colored bill and light orange-colored legs. 2. Probably about five days. Much depends upon conditions.

Pekin Ducks as Layers.—Are Pekins good layers?

The Pekins will often begin to lay when they are six months old, but for next year the layers should be from ducklings hatched in April, or the old ducks should be retained. It is better to use old females with young drakes, if fertile eggs are desired early in the season next year. Pekins grow very fast and mature early. When they begin to lay, they produce a large number of eggs before they cease.

Dressing Ducks for Market.—How should ducks be dressed for market?

Young ducks are usually marketed dressed, leaving on heads and legs, but some markets require the entrails to be drawn, while others do not.

Turnips for Ducks.—Are turnips good for ducks?

Grow a crop of turnips for ducks, if you intend to raise a large number. On the large establishments, where hundreds of ducks are raised, a principal food for them is cooked turnips, with a small proportion of ground grain. No crop can be grown to better advantage than turnips and in no way can turnips be grown so profitably as to feed them to ducks.

Food for Ducklings.—What is the best food for young Pekin ducklings when first hatched? When they are very young is it best for them to have water to swim in, or only enough to drink?

Soft food, such as cornmeal, bran and ground oats, scalded, four times a day, as much as they will eat should be given. They should also have *finely* cut clover, scalded potatoes, turnips, or a variety of any kind. Give lukewarm water, in troughs. Cold water causes cramps.

Crossing Ducks.—Give some suggestions on crossing ducks.

A cross between the Pekin drake and Rouen female makes the best duckling, as it is white in color, like the Pekin, and has the hardiness of the Rouen. Both breeds are very large and grow rapidly. The white color avoids pin feathers showing when the ducklings are dressed. They are never sold alive, as is the case with the adults. The Aylesbury is also an excellent white duck and nearly as large as the Pekin, the two white breeds making an excellent cross. Always use males of the Pekin, Rouen, or Aylesbury when grading up a common flock. The White Muscovy drake and Pekin female is an excellent cross, giving a very compact carcass.

Duck Diseases.—Are ducks liable to disease as much as fowls?

They are subject to but few diseases. Cramps occur from cold water. Leg weakness comes from damp quarters at night. Apoplexy attacks grown ducks when they are very fat, and they are also subject to vertigo. If attacked by the large, grey body lice on the heads, they will appear apparently well and suddenly turn over on their backs and die. The floor upon which they sleep must be of boards and should be kept very clean and dry. Dampness is fatal to young ducks.

Feeding Ducklings.—How should ducks be fed after twenty-four hours old?

Feed them on a mixture of mashed potatoes, which may be thickened with ground grain (composed of equal parts of corn meal, ground oats and middlings), and give them all the milk they can drink. Scald all the food the first two weeks. After they are three days old, give them meat, chopped fine (or ground meat) mixed in their food three times a week. Chopped grass, cabbage, vegetable tops, clover hay chopped and steeped in water, or any kind of green food may be given liberally. After the second week cooked turnips and ground grain will answer, with a little ground meat. Feed four times a day until they go to market.

GEESE.

Geese to a Gander.—How many geese should be allowed to run with one gander?

Geese pair if sexes are equal, and it is best to have an equal number of both sexes; but four females may be allowed with a gander.

Hens as Mothers.—Is it better to hatch their eggs out under a hen, or to let them hatch and raise their own young?

Is it best to allow the eggs to be hatched under geese, as they are the natural mothers. Hens do not always succeed in hatching geese eggs.

Cost of Raising.—How much does it cost to raise a goose to maturity?

To keep a goose confined, and the food bought, the cost may be anywhere from $1 to $3; but if at liberty the cost need not be more than twenty-five cents.

Geese as Layers.—What kind are the most prolific layers? How many eggs will one lay the first year? How many the second year?

We do not believe there is much difference in the laying qualities of the several breeds. Twenty eggs are a fair average the first year after maturity; but after that it may reach forty, as age makes but little difference after the second year.

Goslings.—When should they be allowed to go in water?

Not until well feathered, as they are liable to be severely chilled if the water is cold.

Egg Production—What is the best feed for geese for egg production?

The best feed is a variety of grain and green stuff. They are very fond of foraging.

The Toulouse.—Is the Toulouse the largest breed?

The Toulouse and Embden are of the same size. The adult gander should weigh 25 pounds.

Feed for Goslings.—What is the best feed for young goslings?

At first give ground grain, mixed and scalded, mixed with chopped onions. After they are a few days old feed anything they will eat.

To Tell the Sex.—How can I tell the sex of geese?

The female has a coarse voice, while that of the male is fine. The male is heavier on the neck, and masculine in appearance.

Water Necessary.—Is a pond or stream of water a necessity in keeping geese?

Geese do best on a pond or stream, and will wander to great distances. They do not thrive if denied a body of water in which to enjoy themselves.

For Feathers and Market—Which are the best feathers and how much will one yield in a year? Which are the best for market and what is their "Standard" size?

The best breed for feathers is the Embden, they being entirely white; but the Toulouse yield the heaviest. The quantity ranges from ¼ to ½ pound a year. The best for market is a cross of a Toulouse gander with an Embden goose. Both breeds attain, at times, the weight of from twenty to twenty-five pounds per single bird.

Selecting Geese—Should I keep the old geese or sell them?

In thinning out the flock of geese, always retain the old birds, as they will often live and breed during the lifetime of a generation. Geese have been known to hatch and raise their young when twenty-five years old. The old geese are not saleable in market, and as they are better layers and more careful mothers than the young geese, the latter can be marketed with more advantage and profit than by selling off the old birds.

INDEX.

www.ingramcontent.com/pod-product-compliance
Lightning Source LLC
Chambersburg PA
CBHW031820090426
42739CB00008B/1348